D1043817

A John Macrae Book

HENRY HOLT AND COMPANY   NEW YORK

NOTES FROM

NEW ZEALAND

A

Book

of

Travel

and

Natural History

EDWARD KANZE

Henry Holt and Company, Inc.
Publishers since 1866
115 West 18th Street
New York, New York 10011

Henry Holt® is a registered trademark
of Henry Holt and Company, Inc.

Copyright © 1992 by Edward Kanze
All rights reserved.
Published in Canada by Fitzhenry & Whiteside Ltd.,
195 Allstate Parkway, Markham, Ontario L3R 4T8.

Library of Congress Cataloging-in-Publication Data
Kanze, Edward.
Notes from New Zealand : a book of travel and
natural history / Edward Kanze—1st ed.
p.   cm.
"A John Macrae Book"
1. Natural history—New Zealand.   2. Kanze, Edward—Journeys—New
Zealand.   3. New Zealand—Description and travel—1981–   I. Title.
QH197.5.K36   1992   91-42051
508.93—dc20   CIP

ISBN 0-8050-1990-1
ISBN 0-8050-2665-7 (An Owl Book: pbk.)

Henry Holt books are available for special promotions
and premiums. For details contact: Director, Special Markets.

First published in hardcover in 1992 by
Henry Holt and Company, Inc.

First Owl Book Edition—1993

Designed by Claire Naylon Vaccaro

Printed in the United States of America
All first editions are printed on acid-free paper.∞

1   3   5   7   9   10   8   6   4   2
3   5   7   9   10   8   6   4   2
(pbk.)

FOR PETER MILLER

ACKNOWLEDGMENTS

Never has a traveler or writer owed so much to so many. Acknowledging all the kindnesses bestowed upon me in New Zealand would require a separate volume. But a few provided so much in the way of food, shelter, encouragement, and companionship that their good deeds must be singled out:

Peter Miller, who met me at the airport, introduced me to the New Zealand bush, overwhelmed me with hospitality on six occasions, and offered me the title to his land; Charlie, Marie, and Brendan Daugherty, who on numerous occasions welcomed me into their home like a head of state, and without whose direct assistance and encouragement my schemes would never have succeeded; Alison Cree and her husband, Marcus Simons, who taught me how to fend off bulls, answered a thousand questions, and sheltered me when I was roofless; Michael Thompson, formerly of Victoria University, who arranged my visit to Stephens Island; Donald and Jill Cooper, who served me roast mutton (the unofficial national dish) and introduced me to the ways of sheep; Henry and Ann Paish, friends, fellow bird enthusiasts, and hosts for nearly a week; Arthur George "Salt Spray" Green, artist, brewer of beer, and retired seaman, who housed me on Waiheke Island; and Stanley Palmer, who after a grueling research trip gave me free use of his home and bathtub, and who presented me with a gift of lithographs, vivid mementos of the New Zealand landscape I will treasure always.

A few institutions also deserve grateful mention: the Victoria University of Wellington, which encouraged my participation in several research projects; the New Zealand Wildlife Service, now incorporated within the N.Z. Department of Conservation, which granted permissions and partial sponsorship for expeditions to Stephens, the Poor Knights, and Red Mercury islands; the World Wildlife Fund, which provided financial backing for much of the research in which I became involved; the New Zealand Consulate in New York, where I was granted freedom to rummage through several shelves of books; the American Museum of Natural History in New York, where the library staff helped me locate rare nineteenth-century zoological journals, and Michael Klemens showed me a tuatara preserved in a jar; and Yale University, which kindly granted access to its renowned Sterling Library.

Max Gartenberg, my agent, helped polish the manuscript, and later he brought it successfully to market. Jack Macrae and Amy Robbins at Henry Holt showed faith in the book, supplied hundreds of helpful critical comments, and helped cast the text in its final form. Debbie Koester, Jeff Parsons, Suzanne Lewis, and Michael Hurrell read and commented on early drafts of the manuscript. To all these people, and to Robin Miller for putting me in touch with his brother Peter, I am grateful.

I also thank my family, my friends, and my travel agent, Ingrid Malmstrom Saldibar. Without their support I might have stayed at home.

CONTENTS

PREFACE

This book tells the story of three journeys to the *other* land down under—New Zealand.

New Zealand is a place of striking contrasts. Within its borders modern cities and prosperous farms coexist with Mesozoic beasts lifted straight from Arthur Conan Doyle's *Lost World*. There are subtropical forests of palms and tree ferns, glaciers, and geysers that rival Yellowstone's. You can gaze at the night sky in New Zealand and watch a flock of imported Canada geese pass before the Southern Cross; in an hour's journey you can travel by automobile from an alpine world indistinguishable from Switzerland (except by a botanist) to a seacoast that could pass for Tahiti.

Few readers in the Northern Hemisphere, I suspect, are familiar with New Zealand's geography, zoology, botany, and history. This is perfectly understandable. New Zealand is a small and peaceful country, far from most of the world's population in linear distance and remote from its daily consciousness. For the most part, New Zealand's climate is mild and so are its politics. Neither generates disasters or controversies unpleasant enough to hold the attention of European and American journalists. In the nineteenth century Anthony Trollope and Mark Twain published accounts of visits to New Zealand, but few northern writers have come after them. Among Europeans and Americans, Australia's compact eastern neighbor is better known for its exports—butter, frozen lamb, kiwifruit, Granny Smith apples, antinuclear activism, whole-language teaching, Edmund Hillary, Katherine Mansfield, the opera singer Kiri Te Kanawa, the mystery novels of Ngaio Marsh—than for its endemic wildlife, Euro-Polynesian culture, fresh air, clear water, and grand scenery.

Rather than try to stuff the obligatory facts and figures regarding New Zealand into my narrative's first hundred pages, I have placed them in a separate section at the beginning. This arrangement is designed to preserve some of the spontaneity of real travel. During the first weeks of a trip, few of us pause every few miles to cram from the *Encyclopedia Britannica*; rather, we do our reading before leaving home.

Most journeys or series of journeys begin with an objective. Mine was to get away from home and to escape a job I no longer found satisfying. At the time, I lived in crowded, overdeveloped Westchester County, the business end of New York State, in the United States of America. I served as resident naturalist of a wildlife reserve. Although one would think that working among plants and animals in a protected woodland would (as occupations go) be rather peaceful, in fact the reserve's organizational politics were stormy. Thus New Zealand's mountains, forests, glaciers, farms, labyrinthine coastline, wildlife, seventy million sheep, and three million allegedly even-tempered natives promised to be everything that my job and habitat were not. Off I went, into the unknown.

To the Southern Hemisphere I carried the usual tourist's longings for good food, potable water, and Kodachrome scenery. I also brought along a secret desire. I aimed to find and to see—not in a zoo but wild and free—three animals: the flightless bird known as the kiwi, of which there are three species (any one would do); a strange and primitive reptile, neither lizard nor snake nor turtle nor crocodilian, known as the tuatara, which lives nowhere else in the world save for a few obscure islands off the New Zealand coast; and at least one of the islands' three rare, endemic frogs. The New Zealand frogs, the last survivors of a nearly extinct lineage, are primitive beasts. They lack vocal sacs and eardrums, make no sounds to speak of, and live under rocks where they are rarely found. The frogs were so elusive that the original Polynesian inhabitants of New Zealand occupied the country for a millennium without detecting their existence. Somehow I got it into my head that if I tracked down these creatures—the kiwi, the tuatara, the frog—I would get to know, far more deeply than the average tourist, a land reputed to be among the wildest and most beautiful on earth.

So I quit my post, stored all of my possessions, and booked a flight on Air New Zealand. (My policy: always choose the national airline of the country to which you're traveling, because it has the most to lose from a crash.) I set off on a chilly November day. I made three trips to New Zealand over a span of five years. During the course of them I made a flock of personal discoveries, forged rewarding friendships, saw some of the world's most unusual plants and animals, and returned home without permanent wounds or disabling diseases.

A NOTE ON THE TEXT

The original human inhabitants of New Zealand were the Maori. They were Polynesians and spoke a tongue closely akin to that of the settlers of such places as Hawaii, Tahiti, and Samoa.

Maori is pronounced "Mow-ree." "Mow" rhymes with "how." The Maori who occupied New Zealand at the time of European contact were a fierce people with a gentle language. Today the Maori make up about twelve percent of New Zealand's population. Eighty-two percent of New Zealanders trace their ancestry to England and Europe. Most of the remaining six percent are recent immigrants from Samoa, the Cook Islands, Tahiti, and Tonga.

Several Maori words and dozens of Maori place-names appear throughout these pages. Each syllable is pronounced with equal stress, the letter *r* is rolled on the tip of the tongue, and the letters *w* and *h* combine to form a soft *f*, as in Whangarei ("Fang-a-rei"). This is a gross oversimplification of Maori pronunciation, but I hope it will convey some of the beauty of a euphonious language.

About plurals: Maori words are plural and singular at the same time, Noah Webster notwithstanding. One Maori, a hundred Maori; one kiwi, a thousand kiwi; one tuatara, a hundred tuatara. In the text I have made an exception to this rule for a bird, a rather unusual parrot known as the kea. Although "kea" is a proper plural, I never heard a New Zealander say anything other than "keas," so as keas they will appear.

*I*f errors, significant omissions, or distortions have crept into the text, they are unintentional and the responsibility solely of the author.

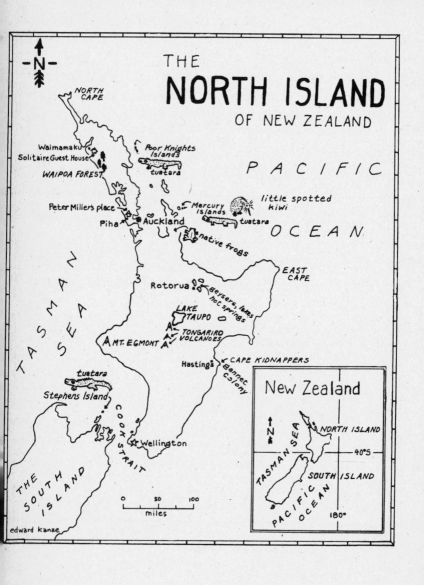

THE

NORTH ISLAND

OF NEW ZEALAND

PACIFIC

OCEAN

TASMAN SEA

NORTH CAPE

Waimamaku
Solitaire Guest House
WAIPOA FOREST

Poor Knights Islands
tuatara

Peter Miller's place
Piha
Auckland

Mercury Islands
tuatara

little spotted kiwi

native frogs

EAST CAPE

Rotorua
geysers, lakes, hot springs

LAKE TAUPO

MT. EGMONT
TONGARIRO VOLCANOES

Hastings
CAPE KIDNAPPERS
gannet colony

tuatara
Stephens Island

COOK STRAIT

Wellington

THE SOUTH ISLAND

0   50   100
miles

edward kanze

New Zealand

N

TASMAN SEA

NORTH ISLAND

40°S

SOUTH ISLAND

PACIFIC OCEAN

180°

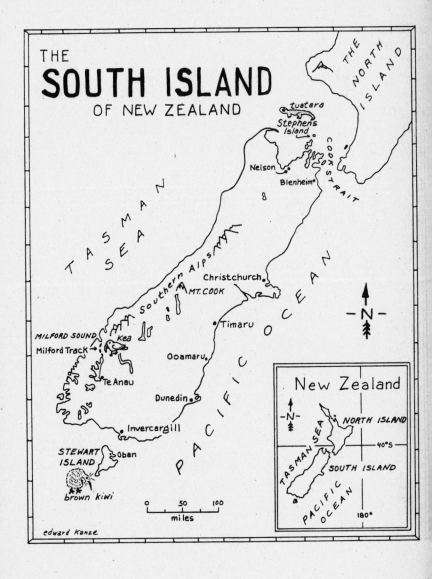

THE
SOUTH ISLAND
OF NEW ZEALAND

THE NORTH ISLAND

tuatara

Stephens Island

COOK STRAIT

Nelson

Blenheim

TASMAN SEA

Southern Alps

Christchurch

MT. COOK

PACIFIC OCEAN

MILFORD SOUND

Kea

Milford Track →

Timaru

Ooamaru

Te Anau

Dunedin

Invercargill

STEWART ISLAND

Oban

brown kiwi

N

0   50   100
miles

edward kanze

New Zealand

N

NORTH ISLAND

40°S

TASMAN SEA

SOUTH ISLAND

PACIFIC OCEAN

180°

NOTES FROM

NEW ZEALAND

A
NEW ZEALAND
PRIMER

*T*hough we say Australia is down under, New Zealand is farther down and under, in fact, than the bulk of Australia. Sydney, which sits well south of Australia's east-west midline, lies at roughly the same latitude as New Zealand's northern extreme, North Cape. Venture south by boat from Hobart, Australia's southernmost major city, and before striking Antarctica you will find little more than water, pack ice, and penguins. Travel south by rail from Christchurch, a New Zealand city at a latitude comparable to Hobart's, and for several hundred miles you'll gaze out upon some of the world's finest grazing land.

Australia, home of Crocodile Dundee and several million kangaroos, lies west of New Zealand. Between the two countries yawns a deep ocean basin. From Melbourne, for example, one must make an eastward voyage or flight of about 1,500 miles to reach Wellington, the New Zealand capital.

The body of water separating Australia from New Zealand is Tasman Sea, known to the Aussies and New Zealanders settled on its shores as the Tasman. The name honors Abel Janszoon Tasman, a Dutch explorer who, on the thirteenth of December, 1642, became the first European to set eyes on the country he called Staten Landt.

Cartographers like to change names as much as explorers enjoy assigning them. In Holland Tasman's charts were set upon by the eraser-wielding geographic establishment. Staten Landt vanished; Nieuw Zeeland (anglicized later as New Zealand) took its place.

New Zealand, almost due south of Fiji, lies about 2,000 miles south of the equator. It is the only land with a temperate climate in all of Polynesia. In virtually every respect—in geography, climate, geology, flora, fauna, prehistory and history—New Zealand and Australia are opposites.

Australia occupies an entire continent and spills over onto a rather substantial island. (The island, Tasmania, covers an area more vast than Massachusetts, Connecticut, Maryland, and Delaware combined.) The Australian mainland is only slightly smaller than the continental United States.

New Zealand, by comparison, is tiny. In dry land it is roughly the size of Colorado or Great Britain. Two islands account for most of the area; they are known, rather prosaically, as North Island and South Island. The north is similar in size to, but slightly smaller than, my home state of New York. The south island is marginally larger than New York. Both the main islands are narrow and elongated. They span their corner of the Pacific end to end, north to south, like one canoe following another. A journey from the northern tip of North Island to the southern tip of South measures nearly a thousand miles.

Australia, by and large, is hot and dry. The country harbors rain forests and forested mountains, but the major portion of the land is, or nearly is, desert. Not surprisingly, the bulk of Australia's human population huddles along its humid coasts.

New Zealand has a mild climate. Nearly all of the country receives abundant sunshine and plentiful rainfall. The north is warm but never hot; the south is cool but never cold. Only at very high altitudes is the climate consistently severe. Australia's trademark color is brown; New Zealand's is green. The islands are as green as Ireland, as green as the jade New Zealand's original inhabitants dug from mines and shaped into tools and jewelry.

If one compares New Zealand and the United States, the northernmost tip of New Zealand is as close to the equator as Greenville, South Carolina, and the southernmost of its cities is as far from the equator as Caribou, Maine. But the climatic differences between North Cape and Invercargill are much less dramatic than those between their North American counterparts. West and upwind of America's east coast lurks a monstrous continent, scorching in summer and bitterly cold in winter. Upwind of New Zealand stretches water. Steady westerlies off the cool, never-cold Tasman make for warm rather than hot summers and mild winters.

In the north of New Zealand the climate is subtropical, and gardeners grow roses and tomatoes all year. On Stewart Island, in New Zealand's far south, snow falls rarely and ponds never freeze. No place in New Zealand is more than eighty miles from the sea.

Geologically, Australia is old and stable. New Zealand, by contrast, is young and impetuous, a country liable to erupt or rumble at any moment. Both of the main islands straddle a fissure between two tectonic plates: the Indian plate, underlying New Zealand in the west, and the Pacific plate in the east. Where the plates grind against each other on North Island, several active volcanoes rise. Where the plates meet on South Island, a range of mountains known as the Southern Alps towers above the sea. The grandest of New Zealand's peaks is South Island's 12,349-foot Mount Cook.

Australia, botanically speaking, bristles with more than 500 species of plants of the genus *Eucalyptus*. Many grow to the size of trees; most, with varying prefixes, are called gums. Eucalypts are as emblematic of Australia's flora as kangaroos and koalas are of its fauna.

Not a single species of eucalyptus is native to New Zealand, although several grow there today, thanks to man. Instead, the flora consists largely of endemics—plants found nowhere else. The monarch of New Zealand's vegetable kingdom is the *kauri*, a gargantuan tree exceeded in size only by the giant redwoods of California. The *nikau*, the country's lone species of palm, grows closer to Antarctica than any other palm in the world. (This is a significant feat, because palms are chiefly tropical and subtropical.) Among New Zealand's plants, many—ten varieties of tree fern, primitive conifers known as podocarps, southern beeches, the kauri, and others—are dead ringers for plants that lived over a broader area one hundred million years ago.

The contrast between Australia and New Zealand is most stark when one compares the animal life of the two lands. At last count, Australia was home to about 230 species of native mammals. Among these are three egg-layers (the platypus and two types of echidna), 110 species of marsupials, and an assortment of rodents, bats, and dingoes. Kangaroos in all their myriad shapes and sizes are unofficial national mascots. Madagascar has its lemurs, Australia its kangaroos.

New Zealand, on the other hand, has no native land mammals. *None.* When man arrived, three species of bat patrolled the air, seals and sea lions lounged along the coasts, but not a single furry creature roamed the interior. It isn't that New Zealand is an inhospitable place for mammals. To the contrary, creatures with fur and mammary glands find the climate agreeable. Today, the wilds of North and South islands teem with rats, cats, brush-tailed possums, wallabies, deer, moose, elk, and wild boar, not to mention more than a few feral sheep, cows, and goats.

The absence of mammals before humans appeared on the scene had to do with isolation. New Zealand drifted away from neighboring continents so early on (nearly one hundred million years ago, according to most estimates) that terrestrial mammals, johnny-come-latelies on the zoological scene, never had a chance to gain a foothold. Once New Zealand was off on its own, the oceans surrounding it functioned very effectively as a moat, keeping mammals out. Until the first Polynesians washed ashore a thousand years ago, only airborne and seagoing species managed to penetrate the defenses. Then the picture changed swiftly. The Polynesians arrived, importing, in addition to themselves, the dog and the Pacific rat.

Before Polynesian settlement in New Zealand, other life-forms thrived in the mammal-free environment. These included many that had died out in places where mammals, which as predators were far more efficient and rapacious than their evolutionary forebears, had proliferated, dispersed, and diversified. As mammals conquered the globe, thousands of slower, less fecund species vanished.

Meanwhile New Zealand, alone in the Pacific and free of

mammals, became a lost world, a living museum of ancient, less competitive species whose near kin had died out on the continents. Among these were primitive frogs whose only known relations live in the northwestern United States and Canada (relics, all, of a time when New Zealand and America were joined to a single great landmass geologists call Pangaea) and reptiles called tuatara. Tuatara look like some sort of spiny, pig-headed iguana. (In Maori, the name means spiny-backed lizard.) Actually, the tuatara is the sole surviving example of an entire order of reptiles that flourished before (and during) the heyday of the dinosaur.

The list of New Zealand's throwback animals is lengthy. Several birds are among the most noteworthy.

Everyone has heard of the kiwi—the bird on the shoe polish tin, the bird that lent its name to the Chinese gooseberry, aka the kiwifruit. Along with a substantial number of other New Zealand birds extant and extinct, kiwi are flightless. There are three species.

Kiwi are odd birds by any standard. Sporting piddling remnants of wings and no traces of tails, they strut through New Zealand jungle in feathers so skimpy and attenuated that together they resemble fur. Scientists are not quite sure if kiwi have close living relations, although the ostrich, the emu, and the rhea are suspected kin. For lack of any place better to put them, they are classed with these birds as ratites. Scientists also wonder: did kiwi ancestors walk to New Zealand when it was part of a greater landmass, or did they fly there, abandoning their wings and power of flight after they arrived? No one can say.

New Zealand is also home to a flightless parrot (a huge thing, called the *kakapo*, nearly extinct) and two species of flightless rail. But the greatest of its flightless birds were the moa, of which there were about a dozen species. All the moa are extinct.

Moa were the largest gravity-loving birds ever to walk the earth. Of them no less an ornithologist than Mark Twain (who visited New Zealand in 1895) wrote:

> The Moa stood thirteen feet high, and could step over an ordinary man's head or kick his hat off; and his head, too, for that matter. . . . It was wingless but a swift runner. The natives used to ride it. It could make forty miles an hour, and keep it up for four hundred miles and come out reasonably fresh. It was still in existence when the railway was introduced to New Zealand; still in existence, and carrying the mails. The railroad began with the same schedule it has now: two expresses a week—time, twenty miles an hour. The company exterminated the moa to get the mails.

Twain, of course, is pulling our legs. It is true that moa were tall and fast and eaten by people, but their exterminators were not railroad men but Maori and their rats and dogs. Using spears, New Zealand's Polynesian settlers hunted the big birds with great success. The last moa were gutted and barbecued shortly before the arrival of the Europeans.

Why did New Zealand harbor so many flightless birds? Probably the main reason was its lack of mammals. In an environment where the ground was free of furry predators, birds lost their weak, porous bones and massive flying muscles and evolved features typically associated with mammals—enormous size, for example, and sturdy legs for running. They also had no need to worry about snakes.

Speaking of snakes: Australia is crawling with them. An unusually high percentage of Aussie snakes are venomous. New Zealand is bereft of snakes. The authors of New Zealand tourist literature boast of this gap in the fauna, banking on the assumption that North American and European travelers are serpentophobic. (Perhaps they are; only we naturalists, I suppose, are disappointed.) New Zealand customs agents work to keep snakes from entering their country as vehemently as the American FBI battles the importation of drugs and suspected radicals. Even New Zealand zoos are snake-free.

Metaphorically, the first snake to enter New Zealand's Garden of Eden was man. Polynesian boatmen (and boatwomen, apparently, for they multiplied) began turning up on New Zealand shores just before the end of the first millennium a.d. Whether they arrived intentionally or accidentally is not known; probably both.

The first people to settle Australia by sea were met by an ancient race of men so intimately associated with the environment that they were practically indistinguishable from it.

The first Polynesian sailors to arrive in New Zealand were met by no one. When they stumbled out of the surf, their footprints were the first by humans ever to punctuate New Zealand sand. Some if not all of the early settlers thrived. The new land, from a Polynesian standpoint, was a mixed bag. A cool climate, especially in the south, made growing the *kumara*, or sweet potato, difficult, and there were no mammals to kill and eat. (Later arrivals made up for this deficiency by introducing, chiefly as food sources, the dog and the Pacific, or Polynesian, rat.) On the other hand, nutritious fern root was widely available, and birds, including flightless and near-flightless varieties, were everywhere for the taking.

By the time Abel Tasman scudded over the horizon in

1642, the Polynesians had created what in European eyes was a rather advanced civilization. True, they used stone tools no better than those of Australian aborigines. But unlike their seminomadic neighbors across the Tasman, the Maori (as the original New Zealanders called themselves) lived in elaborate fortified towns with neat central greens. They carved out of wood council houses and canoes of remarkable beauty and sophistication.

Early European visitors—notably James Cook of England in 1769 and Marion du Fresne of France in 1772—found the Maori attractive and intelligent. The assessments of these explorers may have been influenced by racism, for the highly regarded Maori were lighter in color than the poorly looked-upon Australian aborigines, who were black like sub-Saharan Africans.

Whatever his reasons, Cook described the Maori who greeted him as "stout well made men" and treated them with respect. Julian-Marie Crozet, du Fresne's second in command, found the Maori a "fine, courageous, industrious, and very intelligent race."

That, by and large, is how Europeans saw the Maori. The Maori looked upon the Europeans in an entirely different light. Beneath the strange clothing and light skin, the Maori saw protein.

Social carnivores, the Maori had long been accustomed to eating each other. Therefore it was only natural that when the Europeans appeared in their sailing ships, the Maori saw them as a fresh source of chops, ribs, and loin.

The first European to make the ultimate contribution to Maori cuisine was a Dutchman, a member of Tasman's expedition. Off the shore of South Island, natives in canoes approached a ship's boat and killed three sailors. The Maori were driven off but managed to escape with the corpse of one of the sailors. Although the ultimate disposition of the corpse will never be known, it is likely that it was taken home for supper.

Horrified at the ghastly event, the Dutch named the placid cove where the fracas took place Murderer's Bay. Having seen enough, they hauled up anchor and sailed away.

In 1773 during Cook's second visit to New Zealand, an entire landing party of English sailors disappeared. Searchers went to investigate. They found a shocking sight: "the Heads, Hearts, and Lungs of several of our people ... lying on the Beach; and, at a little Distance, the Dogs gnawing their entrails." Further snooping turned up baskets filled with roasted flesh and fern root, as well as a loose head and a pair of unattached hands. One of the latter, tattooed "T.H.," belonged to Thomas Hill, one of the missing sailors. The head was that of the personal servant of Lieutenant Tobias Furneaux. Furneaux commanded Cook's sister ship, *Adventure*.

English flesh notwithstanding, French sailors made the most generous contribution to the Maori diet. Under the command of Nicholas Thomas Marion du Fresne, the French ships *Mascarin* and *Marquis de Castries* sailed into New Zealand waters on the twenty-fifth of March, 1772. Explorations and a month of peaceful intercourse with the natives of the Bay of Islands followed. Then, on the twelfth of June, du Fresne and twenty-nine men went ashore. Their plan was to visit a Maori village and establish contact with its chief. By nightfall not a single member of the group had returned.

The following morning an armed party investigated. In a hut in the village the searchers found du Fresne's shirt, caked with blood, and nearby, a roasted smorgasbord of legs and entrails. The thirty missing men, it was concluded, had been clubbed, butchered, cooked, and partly devoured. Historians theorize that the French unwittingly violated a *tapu* (taboo). Perhaps they failed to pay proper respect to a chief or burned a sacred object in a campfire. Either way, apparently, New Zealand's Maori did not take faux pas lightly.

In 1809 on the north island, Maori warriors killed and devoured nearly the entire crew (seventy men, including the captain) of the British ship *Boyd*.

Such episodes went far, of course, in dampening European interest in New Zealand as a prospective colony. It is easy to understand why Australia, despite its much harsher climate, was settled first.

The first shipload of Australian immigrants stepped ashore at Botany Bay, near the present site of Sydney, in 1788. A quarter century later, in 1814, the first brave missionaries ventured ashore in New Zealand's Bay of Islands. Little came of their visit, however, and another twenty-five years passed before England summoned the courage to colonize New Zealand in earnest.

Then in the spring of 1839 a group of well-heeled Englishmen joined forces to found the New Zealand Company, a corporation whose goal was to develop the New Zealand wilderness for profit. In May of that year the company sent forth a ship, *Tory*, commanded by Colonel William Wakefield. Carrying an abundance of food, trade goods, and more than a thousand aspiring settlers, *Tory* bustled like a colony of bees seeking a new hive.

William Wakefield was not the first of his family to sail for New Zealand. His brother Edward Gibbon Wakefield had launched an earlier, disastrous attempt at colonization in 1825. When the prospective settlers disembarked at the mouth of the Hokianga River, on North Island, they found themselves in the middle of a bloody Maori war. War New Zealand style involved routine dismemberment, barbecue, and cannibalism. The would-be settlers soon saw enough of these quaint local customs and returned home to England.

The 1839 pioneers chose their landing place more wisely. Wakefield brought *Tory* into Port Nicholson, a capacious bay on the southern end of North Island, just off Cook Strait. There the first order of business was negotiating a peace with the locals. This accomplished, Wakefield negotiated a "purchase" of land that included the entire bay and a vast interior hinterland.

The transaction, typical of those between worldly-wise Europeans and unsophisticated natives, was a steal. The Maori chiefs had little idea what the deed they signed represented. Wakefield, of course, wasn't about to give them a crash course in English property law. Perhaps only Peter Stuyvesant, the Dutchman who bought Manhattan Island for twenty-four dollars, has ever struck a better bargain.

Te Puni and Te Wharepouri, the chiefs with whom Wakefield negotiated, had no use for English sterling. Instead they swapped land for bric-a-brac: two suits of "superfine" clothes (one for each chief), one gross of Jew's harps, sixty red nightcaps, blankets, muskets, tobacco, gunpowder, ten dozen pairs of scissors, ten dozen dressing combs, twenty-four handkerchiefs, two thousand pencils, and a few less useful items.

The year 1840 is pivotal in New Zealand's history. Before it, no organized European settlement existed on either island. But in the spring of that year, beside the bay, Wakefield founded a town on his new land. He named it Wellington after the famous duke, not out of sentimentality but because the conqueror of Napoleon was among the expedition's chief sponsors.

Wakefield's settlement struggled at first but eventually took root. Within a decade it grew into a bustling city, and today it is the New Zealand capital.

The year 1840 also brought William Hobson to North Island, to the place Cook called Bay of Islands. Britain had decided to annex New Zealand as a colony, and Hobson, a captain in the Royal Navy, had been designated its first governor. Before he could govern anything, however, formal possession of the country had to be declared.

After landing on January 29, Hobson convened a meeting of Maori chiefs at Waitangi, a village beside the bay. The chiefs, big-boned men with tattooed faces, were persuaded to "sign" a document ceding "to her Majesty the Queen of England, absolutely and without reservation, all the rights and powers of sovereignty which the said confederation or individual chiefs respectively exercise or possess over their respective territories as sole sovereign thereof."

The treaty was an eyeful for a people without a written language. It was riddled with contradictions. For example, the second article, directly opposing the first, allowed the Maori to retain "full, exclusive, and undisputed possession of their lands and estates, forests, fisheries, and other properties" as long as they had a "desire" to retain them.

Forty-six chiefs marked the Treaty of Waitangi, as it became known, when Hobson presented it. Afterward, copies were circulated around the country, and in the end 512 marks were secured. The queen was satisfied. On the twenty-first of May, 1840, she proclaimed dominion over the two main islands. Now New Zealand was officially a colony, and Victoria was its monarch.

Much of the rest of New Zealand history is the usual colonial tale of subjugation, frontier war, broken promises, contagion, and the conversion of primeval wilderness into pasture and cropland. In two important respects, however, the story strays from the standard plot.

First, it shunned the example of Australia, which, as is well known, was developed as a penal colony. For eighty years, from the arrival of the first cargoes of felons in 1788 until the last men in shackles were ferried ashore in 1868, Britain shipped 160,000 convicts to the kangaroo continent. Not all of them arrived alive, and not all who arrived survived. Australia—hot, harsh, and in nearly every way the stuff of immigrants' nightmares—was the Devil's Island of the South Pacific.

New Zealand, as its citizens will proudly tell you, was never a jail, although Arthur Philip, Australia's first governor, once suggested it would make a very good one. (In Philip's eyes, murder and sodomy were the most deplorable of human transgressions. "For either . . . [he wrote in 1787], I would wish to confine the criminal to the natives of New Zealand, and let them eat him. The dread of this will operate much stronger than the fear of death." The plan was never put into action.)

Second, the New Zealand Maori received far better treatment at the hands of their conquerors than did the aborigines of Australia. The native New Zealanders had light skin and therefore in English eyes appeared superior to Australia's black aborigines. They also had elaborate weaponry, ornate ceremonial houses, and grand war canoes, all of which made them seem culturally more sophisticated than the native Australians, who were wanderers, ate grubs, and practiced no conspicuous religion. Europeans did not yet grasp that aboriginal customs were beautifully adapted to life in a hard environment entirely different from New Zealand's.

By 1839, when the first waves of Anglo settlers crashed upon North Island beaches, English society was beginning to revise its old white supremacist philosophies. Opposition to slavery and to the exporting of convicts was widespread and well organized. Respect was growing for the idiosyncracies of other cultures. To put it bluntly, the English who settled New Zealand in the nineteenth century were a gentler, more broad-minded lot than the thugs, opportunists, and zealots who, in the seventeenth and eighteenth centuries, invaded America and Australia.

*B*efore departing on my first trip, I spent a fortnight in libraries studying developments in New Zealand since the Treaty of Waitangi. Much, I discovered, had happened in a century and a half.

Between 1860 and 1870, English colonists and Maori warriors fought often during a period remembered today (by descendants of the victors) as the Maori Wars. The natives learned exactly what they had signed away at Waitangi—virtually everything.

In 1882 New Zealand exported its first frozen meat. This event was of singular importance to the economy of a country that today ships lamb, beef, and seafood all over the globe.

In 1888 author-to-be Katherine Mansfield was born in Wellington.

In 1893 New Zealand became the first of the world's democracies to grant women voting rights. Another quarter century was to pass before America (Land of the Free, Home of the Brave) took the same step.

In 1907 New Zealand became a dominion of the British Empire rather than a colony. New Zealanders gained a measure of autonomy, but their soldiers continued to die in British wars. A year later, Katherine Mansfield emigrated. Again, New Zealand's loss was Britain's gain.

In 1935 a social security act was passed by the New Zealand parliament. Education, health care, and unemployment benefits were granted for all citizens.

In 1947 New Zealand changed its status from that of a dominion of the United Kingdom to that of an independent nation. The friendly separation left in New Zealand's custody a variety of former British possessions in the South Pacific.

In 1967 New Zealand abandoned the pound and created its own decimal currency, the New Zealand dollar.

In 1971 New Zealand went metric. A mile of road now measured 1.6 kilometers.

And in 1972 the Wellington Parliament adopted the Accident Compensation Act. Under its terms everyone in New Zealand (including the overseas visitor) is granted free medical care for accidental injuries. (This was good news for me: I would be arriving without health insurance and was now free to break bones and sever nerve fibers without concern for the price of repairs.)

FIRST TRIP

1.

8:00 A.M., in the air.

A dark shape rises out of the Pacific like a breaching whale: New Zealand!

While I slept we were crossing lines—the equator, the Tropic of Capricorn, the international date line. We left Los Angeles on Saturday evening. Only fourteen hours have passed, but now it is Monday morning.

The island below is overwhelmingly verdant. There are no signs of civilization, just mountains swathed in emerald jungle. Along the coast, waves spill like milk upon empty beaches.

Auckland, 9:00 A.M.

We're safely down. I'm sitting cross-legged on a sidewalk outside the arrivals terminal waiting for a bus. The air feels warm on my skin, and I detect a scent of flowers. It is November, springtime below the equator.

A dark bird, slightly bigger than a robin, sips nectar from an enormous flowering plant in a garden across the drive. The bird makes sounds like a cuckoo clock, fluffing out a lacy frill of white as it sings. Overhead a big sun brightens a sky that is perfectly cloudless.

A strange thing happened in customs. A man in white shirt and short pants (all the men here seem to wear shorts) asked if I had been on a farm lately. Upon answering yes, I was asked to remove my boots. I obliged, and he hurried off with them to an adjacent room. Through the open door I watched him tease bits of soil from crevices in the soles with a dental pick and spray the bottoms with an insecticide. He returned smiling, with the boots and an apology.

"We can't be too careful," he said.

2.

Auckland.

Am I really in the Southern Hemisphere? I'm beginning to wonder. Auckland is home to a McDonald's, its streets are crowded with movie houses showing fresh Hollywood releases, Madonna blares from the doors of record shops, and Visa cards are welcomed in every store. Worse yet, my cubicle at the Sheraton makes me feel as if I'm in Kansas City.

18

I had a scare upon arriving. While I was killing time in the hotel coffee shop waiting for a room to be prepared (I had arrived early, with a reservation), my bags vanished from the place in the lobby where a bellhop had told me to put them. I made inquiries. The bellhop had gone home, and the rest of the staff weren't interested in helping. When the room was ready a half hour later, the bags still had not materialized.

I was worried: not only was my underwear lost, but an arsenal of photographic gear (about six thousand dollars' worth) was missing, too. Searching on my own with no help from the management, I eventually struck pay dirt. Out on the curb, where taxis and people were busily coming and going, my packs were leaning against a bench. Apparently they had been evicted from the lobby like hoboes.

It wasn't the sort of thing to make a solitary traveler from another world feel welcome.

3.

Auckland, 9:50 P.M.

Three days have passed. I'm camped on a bench in the dark, dusty interior of the Auckland rail terminal. My *bus*—the station serves double duty—doesn't leave until after midnight.

I've just spent twenty-four hours as a guest of Peter Miller, a retired seaman and self-described pensioner. He is a fascinating character, a man who has roamed the world and done just about everything—hauled nets off the North Island coast (he was the captain of a commercial fishing boat), drunk bad whiskey in Punta Arenas, Chile, gotten married twice to the same woman, fathered three beautiful children, been twice divorced, driven through my hometown in New York, even crossed Russia on the Trans-Siberian railway.

I was a total stranger to Peter when I called him from my lair at the Sheraton. (He is the brother of a friend of a friend in New York.) He responded warmly, expressing disappointment that I was committed to another night in Auckland, and promised to pick me up at the hotel the following morning.

The next day at seven, a well-preserved robin's egg blue 1961 Morris Minor puttered into the hotel driveway. It stood out among the limousines and shiny taxis like a man in a coonskin cap at a society ball. Out of the car stepped a thin, gray-haired man vaguely resembling the English actor Alec Guinness. He was wearing battered sandals, short pants, a well-worn summer weight sport coat, and a few crumbs of toast from the morning's breakfast. I liked him at once. "G'day," he said. "I'm Peter Miller."

On the way to his house in the mountains west of Auckland, we stopped at a bottle shop to pick up a fifth of Glenfiddich, an expensive single-malt Scotch. "In honor of your visit," Peter said with a smile. "I hope you drink spirits."

I do, at least occasionally, and so did Peter. He showed me how to freebase the whiskey by mixing it with boiling water from a kettle. Lift the glass to your mouth, and alcohol fumes flood your nostrils. By bedtime the bottle was dry.

Peter occupied a cozy, one-story cabin with an old cat named Butzy. The house had an iron roof and sat within a patch of close-cropped lawn surrounded by dense jungle. Heat (for cooking as well as warmth) was provided by a wood-burning cookstove. Tap water drained by gravity from a cistern filled by rain running off the roof. A short walk away an outhouse, walled in by a palisade of tree fern trunks, perched at the brink of a steep embankment. In front of the cabin, through a cutting in the jungle, a view opened westward to the vast, shimmering Tasman.

Peter owned seven acres of what he called bush, inherited from his father, Monty Miller, who surveyed the area for the New Zealand government when it was still wild. Monty Miller built the cabin in 1924.

We arrived in the Morris at midmorning. By lunchtime we had had two whiskies apiece. "Shall we have another spot before I show you the tracks?" Peter asked. I knew local English well enough to understand I had been offered a refill and a tour of Peter's footpaths. Eager to be a good guest, I accepted both.

On the walk, Peter led the way. The jungle was cool, dark, and mysterious, so I was grateful to have a guide. Up and down precipitous slopes we walked, covering a distance that seemed like miles although we never ventured outside Peter's seven-acre bailiwick. The tracks conquered the steep terrain via numerous switchbacks.

The bush—or forest, or jungle, or whatever it is properly called—was like nothing I'd ever seen. There were dozens of species of trees (Peter, a self-taught botanist of the first order, rattled off the names in Maori as well as in English), nearly all festooned with perching plants, or epiphytes. In fact, to my astonishment, a great many of the epiphytes sprouting from crotches in the larger trees were trees themselves.

There were shrubs, too, of great variety, and an abundance of ferns. Some of the ferns were tree ferns; several stood fifty feet high. Under them, blanketing every square inch of rock, trunk, and fallen log, were low-growing plants I recognized as mosses, lichens, and liverworts.

We passed a lone wildflower, a pale, delicate orchid growing by the edge of a track. There must have been other flowers, however, for the air was scented with a fragrance that reminded me of vanilla.

Peter's tracks were built of mahogany-colored gravel—he called the paving material metal. Beside them streams rushed through dark channels between moss-carpeted boulders, footbridges spanned the streams, and clearings popped up where I least expected to find them. In the open areas, Peter was cultivating vegetables.

At one point we came to a small pond, about half the size of a tennis court, where the water was black like ink. A brook trickled toward one end, while directly opposite was a low concrete dam. Near the dam was a little wooden bathhouse, and along one shore of the pond a shiny aluminum slide led out of the jungle. Peter explained that the little reservoir served as his warm-weather bathtub.

At the bottom of a track leading along the edge of a ravine, Peter vanished. I saw that he had descended a long wooden ladder. Following carefully, I found myself in a cool, leafy grotto. In the middle, beside a quiet, transparent pool, a sign was fixed to a tree:

TENAKOE · TENAKOE

Let all you pigeons and taniwhas,
Glowworms and geckos
Umbrella ferns and Prince of Wales
Feathers, all you rimu and nikau

The water running over the rocks,
Stop and marvel at our wonderful
Cousin Peter and his friend Butzy
Who opened up your secret part
of the Monty Miller memorial park
To let in light and us

With te aroha in our hearts and
Recognition of her generosity
And inspiration these ten steps to
Fairyland are dedicated to
Patricia Miller and her
Beloved Wani

JUDE MILLER 1983

Later that afternoon, after we had returned to the bungalow and tossed back several spots, I ventured out on the tracks alone. Peter was napping.

I feared at first that I might never find my way back. The paths crisscrossed often, and the trees, which might have served as landmarks, were alien and much alike. The bush surrounding me was wet, dark, and pungent.

Where, I wondered, were the birds? All I saw were New Zealand pigeons—wild birds, much larger than the domesticated sort—beating through the treetops with a great whirring. As pigeons go these were beautifully colored, their heads an iridescent blue-green, their enormous bellies alabaster, their eyes and bills and legs a brilliant cherry red.

I heard the calls of birds I could not see. Peter had identified one of them by sound: the gray warbler, or *riroriro*. The song, a melancholy, drawn-out trill, struck me as plaintive and tragic. "I will love you always," the disembodied riroriro seemed to sing, again and again.

At six Peter and I sat down to "tea"—the evening meal. We ate steaks and stewed tomatoes and drank warm milk from a pint bottle. The milk tasted not as if the milkman had delivered it that morning, but rather as if it had been squeezed from a cow only a moment before.

Peter and I were pleased to find that we had much in common. He was fascinated by wild plants and animals, and so was I. He advocated simple living; a week before, I had vacated an apartment that I'd heated for four winters with a wood-burning stove. He distrusted governments and big corporations and believed in passing his days as he pleased, according to his own principles; I, who had just surrendered a job with regular paychecks and a pension plan, seconded the motion.

After supper Peter served coffee and lit a hand-rolled cigarette. We continued talking late into the night. Sometime around ten I asked about tuatara, kiwi, and frogs. Had Peter seen such beasts?

Never a tuatara or a kiwi, he said. Only in zoos. But he had encountered the native frogs. The cat sometimes brought them home.

I was astonished and disheartened. If this man, who had lived in the New Zealand bush all his life and had gotten to know every knob of rock on the North and South Island coastlines, had never seen a tuatara or kiwi, what were my own chances? The prospects for finding a native frog weren't much brighter. Butzy, Peter said, hadn't pranced into the cabin with one in years.

New Zealanders, according to every scrap of tourist literature I had read, referred to themselves as Kiwis. I found this hard to believe, and before turning in to bed I asked Peter if it was true.

"Bugger it, *no*," he said. "That's all nonsense, cooked up by businessmen and politicians. Originally Kiwi referred, I think, to football players—soccer players—but became a label for New Zealand soldiers fighting in Europe. This business of calling ourselves Kiwis today is nothing but pure bloody commercialism."

"What *do* you call yourselves, then?"

"I don't suppose we really have a name."

"Would you call yourself a New Zealander?"

"Oh no, that wouldn't be right at all. Only the Maori can really call himself a New Zealander. I suppose we must be called Pig Islanders. During the war, when everyone else insisted on calling us Kiwis, the Aussies [he pronounced it "Ozzies"] were saying that we were Pig Islanders. They didn't mean it to be flattering, I suppose, but it was a name I rather liked. It's a hell of lot better than"—he spit the last word out with disdain—"Kiwi."

Why Pig Islander?

"As you've undoubtedly learned," Peter said, "Captain Cook put pigs ashore on these islands. His idea was to turn New Zealand into sort of a larder for sailors on future expeditions, and to provide food for the natives. He succeeded, but too bloody well as it turned out."

At eleven (ten everywhere else in New Zealand, but Peter refused to accept daylight savings time), I excused myself and crawled off to bed. I was set up in a comfortable guest bedroom at the end of the house farthest from the chamber where we had eaten and talked. In between was a bunkroom where Peter slept. There was a bookshelf containing old *New Yorker* magazines, dusty Frank O'Hara novels, and a faded issue of *Play-*

boy. Thanks to the whiskey and the rain drumming on the roof, I fell asleep easily.

It was raining still when I woke up in the morning. Peter walked in with a cup of tea and a plate of buttered toast. "An old New Zealand custom," he explained.

———

4.

Hastings.

After leaving Peter's I traveled northward from Auckland as far as I could go. I eventually reached Cape Reinga, one of the three prongs making up New Zealand's northernmost extension. Standing by a white lighthouse that nearly blinded me in the midday sun, I looked north into the sea. A line of foam stretched toward the horizon. West, left of the line, lay the Tasman Sea, its waters a brilliant aquamarine; right, in the east, lay the indigo South Pacific. The foam was produced by the clashing of waters that differ in temperature and salinity.

To get to Cape Reinga I had traveled through Waitangi, the village where the treaty ceding New Zealand to the English was put before the Maori. I had also passed several days relaxing and searching for birds in and around a village called Paihia.

Paihia fronts on the scenic Bay of Islands, among the most popular spots in New Zealand for domestic and overseas tourists. I was surprised to find the village quiet and free of traffic. Ostentatious, expensive hotels were lacking, and several of the local restaurants closed on weekends.

Inland from Paihia is an extensive forest reserve. I tramped there on successive days at dawn and dusk, hoping to find kiwi, but each time I failed. Stealing a look at the national mascot was not going to be easy.

Yesterday I arrived in Hastings, the culmination of a two-day bus trip. An attractive rosy-cheeked woman at the Hastings Tourist Bureau found me a room at the Grosvenor, a homey one-story brick hotel that was clean, safe, and functional.

This morning I caught a bus. It picked me up at the central terminal and dropped me off at the end of the line, at Clifton. A few feet beyond the bus stop pavement gave way to dirt and pasture. Two male New Zealanders (despite Peter's strong argument, I couldn't bring myself to call them Pig Islanders) were already waiting. One was a skinny young man with a sallow complexion, the other his bent, unshaven grandfather. By the time a Land Rover arrived to carry us away, we had discussed the latest weather and politics. In the process, we discovered a shared passion for birds.

Our guide and driver was a thirtyish man with a broad, tanned face. He wore a rumpled cotton hat and worked, he said, at Summerlee Station, a 5,000-acre sheep ranch that occupied the bulk of the peninsula culminating in Cape Kidnappers. Taking people to see the gannets nesting on the Cape, he said, was his most pleasant chore.

As we rumbled up rocky tracks, plunged into steep gullies, and forded rushing streams, our teeth rattled in their sockets and our stomachs jiggled like yo-yos. Along the way, hundreds of sheep paused in their grazing to look at us with diffidence.

Eventually we mounted a high ridge. Beyond, a series of bone white promontories of rock extended into the Pacific, as if the peninsula were not a geologic feature at all but the tail of a giant stegosaurus. The summits of the rocks were flattened, and each was crowned with orderly rows of gannets.

The Land Rover stopped beside a low rail fence. I stepped out, astonished. A few feet away at the edge of a cliff, hundreds, perhaps thousands, of white, gull-sized birds were crowded beside each other, sitting upon nests. The birds, which had stout black bills, were so closely packed together that their feathers nearly touched, and they were so numerous that it would have taken an hour to count them. The birds were Australasian gannets.

According to our driver, this place was "the only mainland gannet nesting colony in the world." (The truth of this statement hinged, I suppose, on whether you regard New Zealand as mainland or archipelago. Gannets nest chiefly on islands.) The birds, he said, had arrived late this year. This explained why they were incubating eggs rather than stuffing food into the mouths of chicks.

When away from their nests, gannets sail over the waves in a relentless search for fish. A hungry gannet that spies a bite-sized morsel presents quite a spectacle. No matter how high up—ten feet above the waves or a hundred—it noses into a steep dive like a kamikaze pilot bent on glory. Upon reaching the ocean's surface it plunges fearlessly into the depths. There it either catches its prey straight away or pursues it, swimming like a penguin.

When the Cape Kidnappers gannets make their annual appearance, each female lays a single egg on a simple nest of seaweed. Then incubation begins. With white contour feathers, wings trimmed in black, a gold wash over the nape, and pale blue lines that frame gray eyes like a woman's mascara, a prospective mother or father gannet radiates elegance—even when sitting upon an egg.

During an incubation shift, the incubator holds the egg between his or her feet. It must be a tiresome chore, for twenty-four hours or more may pass between changings of the guard. The feet are webbed and gray-black in color, with vivid green lines running along the toes. The webbing is rich in blood vessels. Blood provides the warmth required for the gannet embryo's development.

When the egg hatches, the gannets become diligent parents. They roam vast distances searching for food, and it is not unusual for ornithologists to find Cape Kidnappers gannets foraging a hundred miles from the colony. Chicks are fed by regurgitation.

When I asked how many birds were we looking at, the driver replied, "Five thousand, almost exactly." I was skeptical, for only a thousand or two were crowded at our feet.

The driver, not irritated in the least that I had questioned him, pointed to the groups of gannets on the promontories. "Look there," he said. I needed no more convincing.

On the ride back along the peninsula we saw many more birds. Gannets, gulls, and harriers cruised across the sky, and in the paddocks where the sheep grazed, we caught glimpses of paradise ducks, white-backed magpies, harriers, and fantails. English birds were also in sight—goldfinches, skylarks, yellowhammers, and chaffinches.

At one point a couple of hares bounded away, and farther on, as we rumbled around a bend, a pair of bewildered goats bolted out of a thicket, threw a terrified glance in our direction, and fled over a ridgeline. The sightings raised the ire of our driver. "Rabbits and goats are a bloody nuisance," he muttered. "As many as we manage to shoot, there's still no getting rid of the bastards." I was reminded of the attitude of American sheep ranchers toward coyotes.

5.

Rotorua, aka Sulfur City.

With its primeval jungles, cheery weather, and youthful architecture (buildings older than the turn of the century are rare), New Zealand seems an unlikely place to acknowledge Queen Elizabeth II of England as head of state. The queen's rule is just a formality these days, although she still visits. Her favorite destination in New Zealand, I'll wager, is Rotorua. It is a town where the British stamp is indelible.

On my first day here I walked to Tudor Towers, a grand old Edwardian bathhouse on the southern end of Lake Rotorua. Built in 1906, it was refitted many years back as a museum and art gallery, and disreputable wanderers like me are now allowed to explore its genteel interior. By the time I strolled up the drive to the entryway, the sun had broken free of clouds and the sky was a dazzling blue. Instead of going in I plunked myself down outside, on a bench overlooking a bowling green.

I had heard of bowling greens but had never actually seen one. This green, defined by a wooden rectangular border, looked like a hybrid of golf course and swimming pool. Its grass was well groomed and fertilized.

Upon the green were bowlers, men in short sleeves and natty white trousers, women in snow white blouses and skirts. As far as I could tell, the idea of the game was to roll an off-round ball the size of a plump grapefruit toward a group of similar balls on the opposite side of the green; the relative positions of these aspherical objects somehow determined the winning of points. I was struck by the decorum of the players. There were smiles and occasional handshakes, but no laughing or clapping.

To my delight a pair of elderly women in bowling attire joined me on the bench. They were amused, in a friendly sort of way, when I told them I had never seen a game of lawn bowls. A pity, they said, it's a wonderful game. Didn't we bowl in America? I explained that we did, or at least some of us did, but indoors, and in a different sort of way. "Tenpins?" Yes. The two women exchanged glances that I took to be looks of sympathy. Next I said that I had little interest in American bowling but that this outdoor game intrigued me. This must have been the right thing to say, for it provoked a warm response and a thorough explanation of rules and strategies.

Rotorua stinks—literally. It is a handsome town, bordered by a long freshwater lake and erected upon a piece of land that is perfectly flat. But it has a rather conspicuous failing: a chronically unpleasant odor. All day, all night, in every restaurant, along every street, the air is thickened by a sulfurous smell, the sort of odor Emily Post advises us never to acknowledge with a groan or comment. It rises from below, out of cracks in sidewalks and the openings of sewers. It enters your consciousness at the start of every day and continues to announce itself at bedtime. The Rotoruans are used to it, I suppose, just as New Yorkers are accustomed to dirt.

Another thing Rotoruans have gotten used to is danger. The city occupies a slab of volcanic rock plugging the mouth of a volcano. It feels strange to stand on a street corner in this busy city, sulfur filling your nostrils, and to gaze out at the low hills encircling the metropolis like wagon trains around a campfire. The fire, of course, is underfoot, and one day its embers will burst into flame and Rotorua will be no more.

Yesterday I visited a so-called thermal reserve just off a broad avenue lined with northern hemisphere trees and pricey steel-and-glass hotels. Very little in New Zealand had disappointed me, but I was nonplussed here. The hot springs, bubbling out of silica terraces shaped like enormous wedding cakes, were striking but gruesome, stained yellow with sulfur and dirty green with algae.

Since I had paid dearly to enter ("four dollars fifty, thanks"), I roamed the paths among the springs and geysers and took in the sights. I watched the Prince of Wales geyser ejaculate, trudged through an "authentic" (reconstructed) Maori village, marveled at the crowds of Japanese and American tourists who trudged along beside me, and visited a museum of native handicrafts.

The museum, as it turned out, was worth the price of admission. I knew that the native New Zealanders were great wood-carvers, and I had admired the vast collection of their handiwork in the War Memorial Museum in Auckland, but it was illuminating to watch a carver at work. The museum functions as a teaching center and gathering place for active artisans, and during my visit a husky, chestnut-skinned man in a plaid shirt chiseled faces into the surface of a massive log. I watched him for an hour, spellbound. His only tools were a big iron gouge and a wooden mallet, both of which he wielded with a light touch and astonishing skill.

In the afternoon I walked to a forest reserve. There a chatty ranger directed me to what he considered to be the reserve's pride and joy: a grove of California redwoods planted at the turn of the century. "They grow twice as fast here," he said, "as they do in the U.S.A."

The redwoods were impressive, but I wanted to see New

Zealand trees, so I walked deeper into the forest. To my surprise, a short stretch of luxuriant bush soon gave way to a vast plantation of trees in rank and file. One section comprising several acres had recently been clear-cut.

The trees in the plantation were pines. Pines are not native to New Zealand, but, like redwoods and Englishmen, they grow tall and strong under the austral sun. These were Monterey pines, *Pinus radiata*, the chief cash crop of the domestic timber industry.

The Monterey pine (which the New Zealanders, reversing the scientific name, call radiata pine) is a three-needled species that exists naturally in a few forests along the California coast. Under cultivation it grows throughout New Zealand, over a range far larger than its natural one. I saw so much radiata pine on the drive from Hastings that I wondered if anything remained of the central North Island bush.

Today I took an exhaustive bus tour of thermal areas outside of town. The scenery was lovely. There were steamy warm-water lakes surrounded by jungle, mountains covered in dense bush, and dozens of geysers. One of the waterspouts was said to have been the greatest in the world at one time, but owing to changes in the water table it was now a has-been.

After lunch we hiked into a narrow valley punctuated by geysers. We followed a stream and soon found ourselves at the edge of a broad, deep lake called Tarawera. From the deck of a launch coughing diesel fumes into the air, a sharp-featured man with a sunburned face shouted greetings.

Among scenic landmarks Tarawera is a fallen star. Until 1886 silica deposits known as the White and Pink Terraces, situated along the shore, were New Zealand's premier tourist attractions outside of the major cities. Visitors came by boat and wagon from far and wide to admire the formations, famed for their pastel colors and elegant curves. Among those who made the geological pilgrimage to Tarawera was the novelist Anthony Trollope.

I thought often of Trollope as we circled the lake in the launch. While his wife waited back in Auckland, Trollope journeyed to Rotorua, toured these steamy basins, and found them beautiful. The White Terrace, in his eyes, was the more grand of the two in form, while the Pink was most memorable for its pools (in which he bathed), and for its views over the surrounding countryside.

Trollope was entranced with the geologic features of the region, but he found its women more appealing still. One evening in Rotorua, the renowned author of the Palliser novels paid a visit to a hot-water pool in which "three Maori damsels were bathing." He was accompanied by a male companion, and both men were dressed in "very light attire." In Trollope's words:

> I crept down into the pool, and as I crouched beneath the water, they encouraged me by patting me on the back. The place was black, and shallow, but large enough for us all. I sat there very comfortably for half-an-hour while they conversed with the Captain,—who was a Maori scholar. Then I plunged into a cold river which runs into the lake a few yards from the hot spring, and then returned to the hot water amidst the renewed welcomings of the Maori damsels. And so I passed my first evening among the geysers, very pleasantly.

As for "the Captain," he published his own account after Trollope's death. He recalled one of the bathers as "a fine young woman of splendid proportions" and told how Trollope had leaned back-to-back with her, remarking, "Well, Mair, this is very delightful, don't you know, but I think I did wisely in leaving Mrs. Trollope in Auckland."

Geothermal activity put the White and Pink Terraces on the map, and geothermal activity obliterated them. On the tenth of June, 1886, a neighboring peak, Mount Tarawera, exploded. The silica deposits were blown to smithereens. A hundred fifty locals and tourists died in the ensuing firestorm.

After the day of gawking and geysering came to an end, I returned to the snug B&B off Fenton Street that served as my base in Rotorua. There I found neither hot springs nor Maori maidens, only an empty bed and a brightly lit television room where several people were watching a film on a video-cassette recorder. The year was 1984, and this was the first VCR I had ever seen.

Intrigued, I sat down to watch. My Dutch-born host and his English-born wife were chatting with a heavyset man. He had a deeply creased face, a prominent nose, and short gray hair. Against the man's chair rested a pair of stainless-steel crutches.

The moment he spoke I knew he was from New York City; his rough-edged drawl could only have been learned in Queens or Brooklyn. We exchanged names and capsule biographies. He was Abe, a retired airplane mechanic, and New Zealand was his home away from home. "I love it here," he added. I saw an anguish in his face that I did not understand.

Eventually Abe explained. He used to visit New Zealand every year with his wife. They camped and fished for trout and always had a wonderful time. During their last visit together, a logging truck had spun out of control and demolished their rented Toyota. His wife, injured grievously, died after a year of suffering. Abe's legs were broken so badly it seemed for a time that he might never again walk. But he worked hard at physical therapy and now moved confidently with crutches.

"I've come back," he said, "because this is a wonderful country. Let me tell you—I've been *everywhere*. New Zealand is the only place I feel at home."

6.

Ngatamariki.

I have spent yesterday and today herding sheep for Donald and Jill Cooper on their farm an hour's drive south of Rotorua. The Coopers are friends of Emily Wood, a professional acquaintance of mine from New York. Emily is traveling independently in New Zealand, and yesterday morning she and Jill met me in Rotorua and drove me out to Ngatamariki.

The station (as a sheep ranch is called hereabouts) consists of hilly pastures cut into paddocks by lines of electric fence. There are a few small outbuildings, an elaborate complex of livestock pens, and a new, one-story farmhouse stocked with the latest modern conveniences.

Donald Cooper, about thirty, is rugged, dark-haired, and tanned. Jill is slender and fair and perhaps the same age as her husband. She has delicate features and a cheery demeanor. Joanna, the Coopers' three-year-old daughter, is a platinum blond.

Shortly after I arrived Joanna led me out to a fenced yard and introduced me to her pet lamb, Polly. She explained that Polly would accompany her to nursery school next week, and that her classmates would bring their lambs. The event, Jill explained, was a traditional New Zealand form of show-and-tell.

I have been thoroughly enjoying my stay here; the Coopers have put me to work. Our job the past two days was to bring in the flock for "drenching." Drenching, I guessed, would involve spraying the sheep, perhaps with a substance to kill lice. I was half right. The sheep were to be given an antiparasite medicine, but it would be administered internally, to kill off worms and flukes. Donald explained that we would round up the flock and drive the sheep into drenching pens.

So we mounted motorcycles and roared off, following a dusty farm track up into the hills. Accompanying us were three sheepdogs. Two were "huntaways," black-and-tan dogs with big feet and husky frames. Donald explained that huntaways were bred for driving sheep over long distances. The third, a "heading dog" more slender than the others, had a black muzzle streaked with white. New Zealand heading dogs are descended from English border collies, with a bit of Australian kelpie thrown in for sturdiness. As their name suggests, they are nimble and intelligent. A heading dog properly trained can make fast work of transforming a disorganized mob of sheep into a flock.

Through a gate we entered a steeply sloping paddock. Dozens of sheep roamed singly and in clumps of twos and threes. Donald hitched the gate open behind us; it would block the sheep from escaping and send them up the lane toward the drenching pens.

"Rev your engine," Donald shouted. "Keep them moving!" From this point on it was all noise and motion. We roared around the fence line, gunning our engines, circling the sheep. Terrified, the flock bolted toward the gate.

In guiding the sheep, the dogs proved their mettle. Barking, nipping, charging at the heels of strays, they worked like four-legged cowboys. The sheep gave in reluctantly and noisily.

Down the lane we went, sheep, dogs, and motorcycles in a swirling cloud of dust. At the holding pens Emily was waiting. When the dogs had nudged the last stubborn ewe inside, she swung the gate closed behind them.

The job was far from over. Now the dogs pushed the sheep one by one into a runway so narrow that only a single animal could pass through at a time. At the far end Donald waited, swinging a gate back and forth to send the ewes one way, the lambs another. It was necessary to separate the big from the small because the dosage of drench varies with an animal's size.

Donald rearranged the maze of rails and runways so that the lambs, still harassed by the dogs, would move into a pen where Emily awaited them with the drenching machine. I didn't envy her the job, but she was ready and eager. At her home in southern New York, Emily raises beef cattle. For her, drenching lambs was probably no more frightening than grooming a chihuahua.

She grabbed the lambs one at a time, thrusting one end of a tube into their mouths. At the opposite end she squeezed a trigger, and into each animal's mouth went the drench. Donald offered to help but Emily declined, professing that she was enjoying herself thoroughly.

When it came time to drench the ewes, which kicked and squealed menacingly, Donald vaulted over the fence. With his physical and moral support, in two hours' time the job was done. Emily was covered with mud and Donald was laughing.

Today was, or would have been, Thanksgiving. Plymouth Rock and Squanto meant little to the Coopers, but Emily insisted we have a feast. Jill offered to cook, and I was asked to name the main course. Should it be turkey, ham, or something else?

"Mutton," I said without hesitating.

Mutton?

"Yes. After three weeks in New Zealand," I said, "it's about time I sampled the national dish. Would it be any trouble?"

"No, none at all," said Jill, still baffled. I explained that I had eaten in a half dozen restaurants since arriving and none had had mutton on the menu. One establishment served lamb—but *that* I could get easily at home.

Jill smiled. "You must understand, Ed, that when a Kiwi goes out to take a meal in a restaurant, the *last* thing on his mind is mutton. In a country with so many sheep, it is a dish one eats a bit too often."

So out of the freezer came a joint from a recently departed ewe. Several hours later, served with potatoes, green beans, and kumara, it made a magnificent meal. In fact, the mutton was so delicious that I accepted a second helping. Everything I had ever been told about the stuff back in the States suggested that mutton was the toughest, gamiest, least desirable of meats, but the tender, delicately flavored roast I devoured at the Coopers' proved the notion false.

Donald and Jill watched me with quiet amusement.

"This is the first mutton I've ever had," I said. "It's wonderful."

A brief silence was followed by laughter. "Ed," said Donald with a grin, "you've come to the right place."

This morning I drove with Donald in his "ute" (pickup truck, short for utility) to a neighboring farm where Angora goats were being sold. During the ride Donald explained that sheep farming was not as lucrative as it once had been. The government was withdrawing various subsidies, and competition with Australia in selling wool and lamb was growing ever more keen.

Farmers, he said, were turning to new ways of working the land. A great many were raising deer because venison fetched high prices, especially in western Europe. Deer farming was also attractive because it was something new, and competition among farmers was still relatively light. Another venture that was catching on was the raising of Angora goats. The price of specialty wools was climbing, and Angora was leading the pack.

The drive took us along a metal road that ran up the bottom of a valley. On both sides were green pastures, dark and wet in some places, glaucous and dry in others. To the south a few low hills rose gently above the sward.

It amazed me to think that this area was, until a few decades ago, a wilderness. Now, in place of tree ferns and nikau, European grasses feed European sheep. There were few traces of native bush, and one could be easily fooled into thinking this had been pastoral land for centuries. Somehow the English-descended farmers had managed to erase New Zealand and replicate Yorkshire.

While Donald negotiated a purchase with a plump, sturdy man who had emerged from a shed, I wandered off for a walk. At the edge of a grassy area I was blocked by electrified wire. Beyond, an English skylark flew out of high grass, ascending with steady wingbeats up into the cobalt blue, until it turned and came plummeting back to the dusty turf.

The rest of the day was devoted to another round of drenching. In the evening Donald suggested I take advantage of the last hour of daylight by riding a motorcycle up to the top of a nearby hill.

For half an hour I rattled along a bumpy farm track, stepping out of the saddle every few minutes to open and close a gate. The track in several places was fringed with trees—from Europe Lombardy poplars with fluttering leaves, and from America cottonwoods that reminded me of riverbanks where they grew back home. It was dark at the base of the hill. The road, rocky and deeply furrowed by runoff, climbed steeply into shadows.

Up and up I roared and rumbled. On one side of the track the land fell off precipitously. Suddenly I emerged from evening gloom into sunlight. A view opened southward over pine plantations and pastures that looked like green velvet. The summit itself, protected from hungry sheep by a ring of barbed wire, was awash in California lupine, its blossoms, the color of fresh eggs and butter, packed together along the branches like snapdragons. The glow of the flowers matched perfectly the amber sun in the west.

Surrounded by North American wildflowers, gazing into a European landscape, I felt as if faraway places—California, England—were close at hand, while New Zealand, land of kiwi, home of tuatara, refuge of ancient frogs, was farther off than ever.

7.

Wellington.

Today, in the heart of this big city, I saw a penguin.

I had just emerged from my snug cell in the Railton Hotel, a clean, serviceable place on upper Cuba Street, just off Wellington's central mall. Breakfast came with the price of the room, and this morning it consisted of greasy sausage, leathery slabs of fried ham, scrambled eggs, brick-hard toast, jam, and peaches adrift in syrup. About a dozen other guests had gathered in the vast dining room, sitting in clusters of two and three. They spoke in whispers, as if they all knew each other. (Perhaps they did. The Railton, run by the Salvation Army, is the biggest bargain in town and boasts a faithful, if threadbare, clientele.)

Now, at 11:00 P.M., I sip Steinlager from a can I smuggled past the desk clerk. Downstairs "The A-Team," the quintessentially American television series about heavily armed vigilantes who roam the world righting wrongs, is playing loudly in a lounge. The program leads the national ratings.

Birds were the last thing on my mind this morning when I ventured out of the hotel and marched down Cuba Street. Gone were the noisy armies of skinheads and punk rockers that had dominated the scene when I arrived after dark. Now there were housewives with children in tow, bustling in and out of grocery stores, and well-scrubbed fortyish men and women in natty business attire, swinging expensive briefcases. I joined the throng and, working my way toward downtown

Wellington, poked into shops specializing in cheap housewares, polyester clothing, and dog-eared paperback books. A block from the hotel, workmen were demolishing a section of Cuba Street with jackhammers.

I came to a cross street upon which electrified buses were playing follow the leader. To the right I could see an early lunchtime crowd fighting its way into a McDonald's. I continued ahead and the street grew quiet. Empty cars lined the curbs, and the shops of upper Cuba Street were replaced by glass-and-concrete office towers of the sort that drain color from modern cities everywhere. At last I found myself on a pier. Here big oceangoing boats were engaged in intercourse with a tangle of cranes, ramps, and lorries.

So this was Port Nicholson. Far out, looking across the vast natural harbor, I could see a small, low island. Beyond, on a distant shore, I could make out the hazy forms of houses that lined the shore of the bay. Behind the houses, forested mountains loomed like a painted backdrop.

As I took in the view, I happened to glance at the murky water. There to my surprise I saw a creature bob abruptly to the surface, as if it were an inflated toy that had been held underwater and suddenly released. It was about the size and shape of a small woodchuck, except that it had a bill, and its color was gunmetal blue like the water.

With a loud gasp the animal took a hurried breath and plunged back into the brine. Then I realized what I had seen. The apparition was a bird—a penguin. It was a little blue, the smallest penguin in the world.

Fifteen species of penguin grace the southern seas, and thirteen of them have been recorded in New Zealand. Of these, three nest along the mainland coast: the little blue, the yellow-eyed, and the Fiordland crested. I was hoping to see at least one of these during the course of my journey, but I had imagined an encounter on some remote beach or inaccessible headland—not some gap between two merchant ships in Wellington harbor.

Sighting the penguin was a breakthrough, as was the telephone conversation I had a few minutes afterward. At last I had made contact with a New Zealand wildlife expert, someone who might help me find tuatara, kiwi, and native frogs. I spoke with Dr. Charles Daugherty, a zoologist at the Victoria University of Wellington. A transplanted American, Charlie (as he insisted I call him) earned his undergraduate degree at Middlebury College in Vermont in 1968, just as I had done ten years later. Before leaving the United States, I had been given Charlie's address by one of my college classmates. I wrote to him in New Zealand, describing my zoological interests and travel plans. He replied without delay, urging me to look him up when I arrived.

On the telephone, Charlie was friendly and funny. He said he would be happy to talk with me about seeing some of New Zealand's elusive wildlife, and we hatched a plan to meet the next day.

8.

Cook Strait, aboard the Aratika.

A cool salt breeze caresses my face, which is warmed by midday sunshine. Bound for South Island, I'm sitting in a molded plastic chair on the upper deck of a ferryboat, somewhere in the middle of Cook Strait.

I met Charlie and Marie Daugherty on Sunday as planned. Perhaps because he is a scientist (a geneticist), I had expected to find Charlie austere, in spite of his warm manner on the telephone. I feared he might give me the third degree about my knowledge of New Zealand's wildlife, which was sketchy. But I need not have worried. He was pleased by my interests and eager to provide encouragement.

Marie Daugherty also provided a friendly welcome. Like Charlie, she is an American. The Daughertys met during their university days, got married, and have lived in New Zealand for several years. Marie is a nurse at the university where Charlie does his teaching. Any day now she will give birth to the Daughertys' first child.

Our initial meeting was brief because the Daughertys had to hurry off to another appointment. Before we separated, they invited me to join them for a meal at their home in Eastbourne, a Wellington suburb.

The next afternoon I met Charlie at the university as planned, and together we drove to Eastbourne. Over an informal dinner of tacos and domestic Lion Brown beer, we talked about the animals I was hoping to find in New Zealand.

"I wish I could offer you encouragement, or even good advice," Charlie said. "But the truth is, those animals, even for scientists, are extremely difficult to get close to. Kiwi live pretty much only in dense bush. Your best bet to see one, and it's far from a guarantee, is to spend a few days on Stewart Island."

Thirty-seven miles long and twenty-five miles across, thickly forested and thinly populated, Stewart Island lies just off the southern extremity of South Island. It is, except for one small fishing village on the east side, a vast reserve of native bush.

Charlie filled me in. Because Stewart Island is closer to the Antarctic Circle than the rest of New Zealand, its nights in summer are especially short—so short, in fact, that the island's resident kiwi, normally inclined to be nocturnal, leave their burrows at least some of the time, to root for grubs by daylight. If they didn't hunt in sunshine at least occasionally, the kiwi would starve.

"Even on Stewart your chances will be slim," said Charlie. "Every New Zealander has seen kiwi in zoos, but hardly any have seen one in the wild."

As for my chances of finding tuatara, Charlie was sympathetic but even less hopeful. The slow-moving reptiles, extirpated on the mainland, live only on offshore islands—about thirty islands, all told. Each of these is guarded as a refuge. Because tourists might unwittingly bring in rodents, cats, diseases, or fire, the islands are strictly off limits.

"Do scientists ever visit the tuatara islands?" I asked.

"Yes, but I'm afraid that no expeditions are planned for this month or next."

Charlie tried to cheer me up. "If you like," he said, "I can arrange for you to meet with Don Newman. Don is a scientist with the Wildlife Service, which controls access to the islands. Over the last ten years Don has had a hand in nearly all of the field research on tuatara, and it's possible he has a trip scheduled I don't know about. At any rate, you'd enjoy talking to him. If you come back to New Zealand someday, having had Don get a look at you can only help your chances of being invited on an expedition."

Charlie was as good as his word. The next day I was sitting in Don Newman's office listening to stories of tuatara.

A slender man with a boyish smile and a tousled thatch of strawberry blond hair, Don was reticent until I began asking questions. Then he launched into a spirited account of his years of fieldwork.

Don, alas, echoed Charlie's doubts. My chances of getting out to an island, this year at least, were nil. For the present I'd have to settle for seeing tuatara in zoos, although if I returned to New Zealand someday, perhaps something could be arranged.

And so, having made new friends in Wellington but gained little ground, I hopped on the interisland ferry. It was a brilliant day. I leaned back and gazed at a squadron of red-billed gulls sailing across an ultramarine sky. Circling the boat continually like runners completing laps, the birds occasionally shifted course and flew over the exhaust stacks. The updraft from our diesel engines sent them rocketing skyward.

Out over the water, skimming the waves, were petrels and shearwaters—plain, dusky birds that lacked the elegance of the gulls. I recognized only one of them: *Daption capensis*, the so-called Cape pigeon. This is a petrel of the southern oceans, and its ample torso, undersized head, and mottled wings are distinctly pigeonlike. Cape pigeons followed the boat, snatching up aquatic creatures churned in the wake.

A mist on the southern horizon lifted, and for the first time I saw South Island. It was as radiantly green as North Island but more rugged and desolate. The native frogs of New Zealand are unable to endure South Island's cool climate—at least none has ever been found there—and the Maori found it a poor place for growing the sweet potato, taro, yams, and gourds on which they depended. Those Maori who did withstand South Island's rigors were hunters and gatherers.

We eased into the calm waters of Tory Channel. Rocky

slopes rose to port and starboard. Then the channel widened and we entered Queen Charlotte Sound.

New Zealand, being a nation of islands, has no Nile, no Hudson. Eighty miles from the sea is the farthest inland one can get; there is no vast basin for a great river to drain. If there were such a river it would not be navigable; because of the narrowness and great height of the islands, the river would be a waterfall. For these reasons the avenues of exploration and early trade in New Zealand were coastal waters and bays.

Queen Charlotte Sound acquired its name in 1770. While James Cook was circumnavigating North Island, proving that it was in fact an island rather than a peninsula on some great southern continent, he sailed into the strait that now bears his name. In passing, he dropped anchor in a quiet bay, which he named Ship's Cove. Beyond, penetrating inland, lay a channel. Cook named it after Queen Charlotte, the wife of George III.

Queen Charlotte Sound made a perfect base. Cook used it to launch exploratory forays along South Island's convoluted northern coast. In the course of these trips Cook traded with the Maori, brewed antiscorbutic tea from local greens (he was a pioneer in the prevention of scurvy), and sent parties ashore to find streams and replenish water kegs.

Encounters with the natives were often shocking. In his journal on January 17, 1770, Cook wrote:

Soon after we landed we met with two or three of the Natives who not long ago before must have been regailing themselves upon human flesh, for I got from them the bone of the fore arm of a Man or a

Woman which was quite fresh and the flesh had been but lately picked off which they told us they had eat, they gave us to understand that but a few days ago they had taken kill'd and eat a Boats crew of their enemies or strangers, for I believe they look upon all strangers as enemies. . . . In order to be fully satisfied with the truth of what they had told us, we told one of them that it was not the bone of a man but of a Dog, but he with great fervency took hold of his fore-arm and told us again that it was that bone and to convence us that they had eat the flesh he took hold of his arm with his teeth and made shew of eating. . . .

On another day Cook and Joseph Banks, the ship's naturalist, encountered a group of Maori transporting dismembered human remains in a canoe. The Englishmen were at once horrified and fascinated. Banks went so far as to purchase a severed head. Afterward, aboard *Endeavour*, he pickled his grisly souvenir so that it could be carried home to England.

One fine morning Cook granted his men a day's shore leave. In those days such beneficence was rare among ship captains; desertion was a constant threat. But Cook knew he had little to fear, for the English sailors had seen what he had seen. None was eager to cast his lot with the Maori.

Leading an expedition in search of a great southern continent, Cook returned to the sound in 1773. For nineteen days he and his sailors lingered, replenishing water supplies, collecting scientific specimens, putting ashore the first pigs and goats ever to sink cloven hooves into South Island sand. Cook sailed away without incident, but near year's end his sister ship

Adventure ran into trouble. The locals pounced, and several sailors were killed and devoured.

Cook last visited Queen Charlotte Sound in February 1777. On this, his third and final Pacific voyage, he intended to fill gaps on nautical charts and to search for a Northwest Passage.

Anchored in familiar waters, Cook allowed visits to *Resolution* by Maori who lived in huts along the shore. One of these, a chief named Kahoura, was the reputed murderer of an English sailor cannibalized three years earlier. Cook accepted the news of Kahoura's presence calmly and allowed him to visit the ship unchallenged. "If I had followed the advice of all our pretended friends," the captain wrote, "I might have extirpated the whole race. . . ."

On February 25, 1777, Cook sailed away. He died two years later, stabbed in a skirmish at Kealakekua Bay, on the island of Hawaii.

We approached Picton, a village with the hastily assembled look of a frontier town. Long piers heaped high with raw timber extended into the bay, and low buildings crowded the waterfront. Beyond the town a circuit of high, stubborn hills loomed, blocking views into the interior.

As we docked I gazed past the ferry terminal to a railroad platform. A train awaited, the one which would carry me along South Island's east coast. The engine and the passenger cars were miniatures. New Zealand's railways are of narrower gauge than those of Europe and America, and their rolling stock is reduced proportionately in size.

The ferry shuddered as its screws reversed. A moment later we struck South Island with a dull thud.

9.

Dunedin.

From Picton I traveled by rail to Christchurch, where I arrived in the early evening. Christchurch is a city of 168,000 (299,400 if one extends the official borders into the suburbs), making it New Zealand's first, second, or third most populous metropolis, depending on whose figures you consult. Often described as the most English city outside of England, Christchurch boasts a grand cathedral, a River Avon, a world-class botanic garden, and an array of shops to rival Kensington High Street.

The very fact of Christchurch's Englishness dampened my interest in it. I had found much of England in New Zealand, but it was the Southern Hemisphere, with its kiwi, tuatara, frogs, and penguins, that I had come to see.

I spent one night in Christchurch, holed up in a cozy guest house where the walls were decorated with emblems and photographs from American Antarctic expeditions. The city is Uncle Sam's gateway to the Far South, a launching place for research parties. I already knew this but was still surprised to find the lounge in a squat brick hotel in Christchurch decorated with the Stars and Stripes.

At times it seemed as if the equator had migrated southward, and New Zealand, with its culture so strongly influenced by Europe and America, now lay in the Northern Hemisphere. All that remained, or seemed to remain, of the Antipodes were rocks, ice, a few penguins, and Antarctica.

The rail journey to Dunedin was uneventful. The train was all but empty. I sat alone for six hours, eating apples and gazing out at farms and seascapes. The tracks ran along South Island's east coast, so we were never far from the Pacific, which struck me, as it always does, as unthinkably vast.

We rumbled through one compact city after another with names such as Timaru and Oamaru, but mostly the tracks carried us across grazing land. The pastures were pancake-flat at the outset but grew hilly farther south. There were countless sheep, a few scattered herds of dairy cows, and broad swaths of cropland. In the west, facing inland, the farms grew thinner and thinner as the slopes grew steadily higher. Eventually they were replaced by jagged mountains dusted with snow.

New Zealand is part of Polynesia, but one would never guess it from the scenes visible from the train. The rolling hills, the pastures, the livestock created an illusion of northern Europe. Only an occasional glimpse of an Australasian harrier—a white-rumped bird of prey—betrayed the geographical truth.

The scenery of eastern South Island left me with contrary emotions. I was aghast at the total destruction of the original environment, yet I had to admire the sheer doggedness of those who took this remote corner and turned it into a perfect replica of their ancestral homeland. Botanists predict that by the year 2000 there will be more alien plants in New Zealand than natives. Already about 1,500 exotics have taken root, and more arrive all the time.

The transformation has been so complete that now English birds thrive in this austral Yorkshire. Among the abundant and conspicuous species are redpolls, skylarks, starlings, house sparrows, chaffinches, blackbirds, song thrushes, and European goldfinches. Homesick Englishmen carried these birds to North America as well, but there for a variety of reasons they perished, except for starlings and sparrows. On the south island of New Zealand they flourished; everything seems to flourish here but the natives.

The transformation from a Polynesian to an English environment was swift. Although European settlement did not begin in earnest until the 1840s, by 1895 the look of the land had been so altered that Mark Twain dubbed the country a "junior England."

Even earlier, during an 1872 tour, Anthony Trollope found the scenery reminiscent of home and the New Zealanders deeply satisfied with the change they had wrought. He wrote,

> The New Zealander among John Bulls is the most John Bull-ish. He admits the supremacy of England to every place in the world, only he is more English than any Englishman at home. He tells you that he has the same climate,—only somewhat improved; that he grows the same produce,—only with somewhat heavier crops; that he has the same beautiful scenery at his doors,—only somewhat grander in its nature and more diversified in its details; that he follows the same pursuits and after the same fashions,—but with less of misery, less of want, and more general participation in the gifts which God has given to the country.

Twain, commenting on the residents of Dunedin, echoed this view: "They stopped here on their way from home to heaven—thinking they had arrived."

We clanked and squealed to a halt at the Dunedin railway station in early afternoon. After checking into a room at the

Leviathon Hotel, I wandered across the street to the Otago Early Settlers Museum. I stepped inside and had a pleasant surprise. Good coffee was scarce in this land of tea drinkers—standard fare here was the bland powdered stuff—yet the interior of the museum was filled with the aroma of freshly ground coffee beans. Some sort of medieval fair was going on, and galleries normally devoted to exhibits were crowded with booths at which costumed merchants hawked woolens, jewelry, and crafts. Lute music played over a loudspeaker, and refreshments were being sold by a gray-haired woman seated behind a folding table. Upon the table was a sign: "Fresh Ground Coffee, Fifty Cents." I dug a heavy coin out of my pocket, Elizabeth II on one side and Cook's *Endeavour* on the reverse.

This morning I hustled back to the museum at opening time, paid another admission fee, and quaffed three cups more.

But albatrosses and penguins, rather than coffee and cream, were the main attractions in Dunedin. At the end of a broad, hilly peninsula jutting out from the city's edge, royal albatrosses nest. They are among the biggest seabirds in the world, and this is their only mainland breeding site. As a bonus, just down the road was a beach where penguins came ashore to nest. The species breeding here was the yellow-eyed, or *hoiho*, as the Maori call it. It is found only in New Zealand and is the rarest penguin in the world.

By bus I was able to reach both nesting areas. My first glimpse of an albatross, the beast that frightened Coleridge's Ancient Mariner, surprised me. I had expected to find the biggest flying bird in the world sinister and forbidding. Instead, seen at a distance camped upon eggs, the albatross appeared gentle and friendly. It was no more intimidating than a gull.

The royal albatross colony sits atop a high cliff at a place known as Tairoa Head. In order to take off from land, these jumbo jets of the bird world (their wingspans average ten and a half feet, and can run to thirteen feet) need a runway and a brink from which to jump. Once in the air, however, they are as graceful as swallows.

I watched an albatross take off and felt a rush of envy. A dozen years before, I had spent a week hang gliding in the Bavarian Alps. I knew exactly what the albatross was feeling as it dropped into the void, the air rushing under its wings and swirling past its face, and that sudden thrill of being aloft. The birds fly to Argentina for winter and return to New Zealand in summer, riding air currents stirred by the waves. They do this year after year, for fifty years or more.

Locating the penguins was more difficult than finding the albatrosses. After riding a bus from Tairoa Head to a bluff above a beach where yellow-eyed penguins come ashore regularly, I scanned the sea and breakers for nearly an hour. I saw gannets and gulls and thickets of California lupine, but no penguins.

The penguins were said to be most visible just after emerging from the surf, during the brief time it takes them to cross the sand before plunging into the bush. Inland they nest alone, not in colonies like other penguins. I watched, and waited, but saw nothing. At last I noticed two dark shapes cruising toward the beach. I was high above the water, so high that I had no sense of scale, and at first I mistook the bodysurfers for humans. But as the surge retreated, leaving a ribbon of foam on the sand, I saw the two figures right themselves. They were penguins.

The birds waddled quickly and deliberately, one slightly ahead of the other, across the beach and up the dune that formed the inner wall of the bay. I watched them through binoculars. Each penguin had a black back and white belly.

The flippers, or wings, were similarly marked, and they swung back and forth as the birds walked, like arms. The bills of the penguins were pink. To be certain that these were yellow-eyed penguins rather than little blues (an abundant species), I looked closely to see if yellow stripes swept back from their vivid yellow eyes. The stripes were present.

Megadyptes antipodes, as this penguin is known to scientists, was once an abundant breeder on South Island shores. But in recent decades its numbers have plummeted—no one knows precisely why. The decline probably has much to do with habitat loss (sheep and other introduced mammals are wreaking havoc in the nesting grounds) and perhaps also with the vulnerability of adults and nestlings to attack by dogs, cats, and weasels. Penguins nest on the ground and are slow-moving out of water.

The penguins trudged up the last few feet of dune. In a moment they were gone.

Now that I'm back at my room at the venerable Leviathon, I have just eaten an informal meal the penguins would approve of—sardines on whole wheat bread—and I am drinking a bottle of Speight's. According to a clerk in the nearby bottle shop, it is Dunedin's favorite beer.

On this warm, sunny evening, I would prefer to wander the narrow lanes of Dunedin, taking in the town's Scottish flavor and admiring its Victorian architecture, the finest in New Zealand. Instead I am poring over bus and train schedules, making plans.

Time (and money) are running low. It is December, and I hope to be back in New York for Christmas. I have seen much of New Zealand; I have looked upon gannets, albatrosses, and penguins; but I have yet to catch glimpses of the sirens that lured me here: the tuatara, the frog, and the kiwi.

Finding a native frog is impossible now: there aren't any on South Island. Seeing tuatara is also out of the question, at least this year. Perhaps I'll come back and settle that score on a future occasion. For the moment, my only real hope (a slender one) is to track down a kiwi.

I am within a day's journey of two places where kiwi still abound: Fiordland National Park, on South Island's mountainous western flank; and Stewart Island, the big, bush-covered island Charlie Daugherty recommended I visit. Seeking a change in luck, I'll travel to both places and spend my remaining days in the bush.

10.

Te Anau.

Rain is falling in Te Anau (pronounced "Tay-Ah-No"). It rained yesterday, and rain will fall again tomorrow. A steady drizzle has cast a veil over the landscape since dawn, and it seems unlikely to lift.

Te Anau village sprawls along the shore of a freshwater lake of the same name. Lake Te Anau is forty miles from end to end. Its waters, cool and deep, teem with trout, imported long ago from Europe and America. Some of the fish grow to immense size.

A retinue of icy streams pour down from mountains flanking Te Anau's western and northeastern shores. Since my arrival the peaks, which are allegedly rugged and snow-covered, have been hidden by rain and fog. The outlet of Te Anau pours through a hydroelectric plant south of the village. Miles downstream it empties into a lesser, but still substantial, lake called Manapouri.

To the west of Te Anau rise the Murchison, Stuart, and Franklin ranges. These mountains are so rugged, so densely forested and wet that few humans have explored them. In 1948 an ornithologist wandering in the Murchison range came across flightless birds—a type of rail—called *takahe*. Fifty years earlier, these birds had been pronounced extinct.

Today at a breeding center for the endangered birds at the edge of the village, I saw several takahe up close. I was struck by their size and color, and amazed that such big, brightly colored creatures could remain undetected anywhere for half a century.

Each takahe I saw was as big as a small dog. Their feathers were iridescent and reflected vivid blues, greens, and violets. Their beaks—red, massive, similar in shape to shears designed for cutting heavy metal—looked well adapted for mincing the tough grasses and sedges upon which takahe feed. Takahe are diurnal; finding them in a high-altitude grassland (their habitat) would seem as easy as spotting a whale in a swimming pool.

The entire western shore of Lake Te Anau (in fact the entire southwest corner of South Island) lies within Fiordland National Park. Except for snowfields and tussock-lands above bush line, the hills and valleys are buried in rain forest.

Tomorrow I will enter the rain forest as a member of an organized hiking party. We will traverse New Zealand's most celebrated footpath, a route to the sea known as the Milford Track. Foul-weather gear, I have been told, is a must. At

Milford Sound, for example, where the tramp will end, nearly three hundred inches of rain fall every year.

In order to acclimate myself (and to continue the search for kiwi), I passed the last several days in Te Anau village. My base was a dry, friendly B&B run by a man named Mike Shakespeare. I arrived soaked and bedraggled, and my host winked as he greeted me. "Would you like a shower," he asked, "or have you already had one?" My fellow guests included two young Texan men and a woman cyclist from Stuttgart.

Each evening at dusk I've wandered the grassy lakeshore and the bush (the term *bush* has room under its umbrella for rain forest) across the lake. I have searched hard and listened intently for a kiwi, but so far I've found only buses crowded with Japanese tourists, dozens of sightseeing planes, and trout. The only wild animal I've seen, aside from the usual bush birds, is an English hedgehog, lying flattened and dead in the road.

I have seen myriad plants. In the rain forest I've spotted southern beeches (genus *Nothofagus*), distant relations of the smooth-barked American beeches in the woods back home. Nothofagus beeches are also found in South America and South Africa, a distribution explained by an ancient fusion of the southern continents. Today I collected samples of three: red beech, silver beech, and black beech. Although the trees here would, if relocated, tower over those in North American forests, their leaves are far smaller; each leaf is no bigger than a thumbnail.

Other samples collected included lancewood, familiar from Peter Miller's North Island bush; miro, a coniferous tree that looks something like yew; and kowhai, which I found growing on a peninsula along the lakeshore. A legume, kowhai is famed for extravagant yellow blossoms that appear in spring. Apparently I've arrived too late; the kowhai are laden with beanlike fruits.

The beech forest is so moist, so crowded with ferns, so thickly cloaked in moss and other creeping growth, that you feel, walking through it, as if you are inside a terrarium. Trunks of lofty beeches stand comfortably apart—they are pillars supporting a great collective canopy of leaves. Underfoot are ground-hugging plants. There is hardly any intermediate layer, what we in America would call an understory. The zone between the upper and the lower is a gloomy catacomb, a place where gnomes and goblins might lurk behind trees.

One evening, while walking back to the village at dusk, I came upon a familiar sight—a flock of Canada geese. There were a dozen of them, all busily tugging on grasses and dandelions. Canada geese were imported to New Zealand as game birds, chiefly in 1905 and 1920. Today they are widely distributed on the big South Island lakes.

11.

Glade House.

A violent shower beats a roll on the iron roof. If someone had led me here in a blindfold, I would guess that I am inside a drum, rather than a cabin.

Yesterday our guide told us to expect three days of rain.

Tomorrow we will tramp ten miles. Tonight, the entire annual rainfall (all twenty-five or thirty feet of it) seems to be descending in one great deluge.

The party of which I am a member was organized by the Tourist Hotel Corporation of New Zealand (THC), a government-managed entity that operates luxury hotels in several of the country's national parks. Because it holds a near-monopoly on the use of the Milford Track (at one point the only legal way to walk to Milford was to join, at considerable expense, a THC-sponsored party), the THC is often discussed in negative terms by New Zealand outdoorsmen. Walkers in THC parties have it too easy, they say. Perhaps there is merit in their argument. We will sleep in heated "huts" (any backcountry accommodation in New Zealand is called a hut, no matter how grand), eat hot meals served in dining rooms, and stow our wet gear each night in heated drying rooms.

I am, it must be admitted, mildly embarrassed to be a THC softie.

Our route will bring us through some of New Zealand's finest wilderness. I hope to find a kiwi here, but there will be plenty of mountain scenery and native wildlife to reward my effort if I do not. I am sure to meet, for example, a parrot called the kea. New Zealand ranchers claim keas, which are no bigger than chickens, kill their sheep. Biologists disagree. Whatever the truth about their feeding habits, keas, the world's only alpine parrots, are unusual birds, and I'm eager to find them.

We gathered this morning outside the sprawling THC hotel in Te Anau village. In all there are thirty-seven of us, hailing from Europe, North America, the South Pacific, and Indonesia. So far among the party I've met a doctor, his wife, and their three teenaged boys from Gainesville, Florida; an engineer from South Australia; a young woman from Singapore; a Californian who could pass for the actress Ali McGraw; a man and wife from Luxembourg; two young couples, neither married, one from Ontario, the other from Chicago; a family of four from South Island whose teenaged son and daughter are forging an instant friendship with the Floridian boys; and a middle-aged couple from New Jersey.

A bus took us to Te Anau Downs, where a boat awaited. It was an old diesel tub named the *Tawera*. Boarding ahead of me was a tall bearded man. He introduced himself as Philip Temple. We were about to travel across the lake, he said, in a boat that had carried walkers to the trailhead since 1898.

The *Tawera* proved lakeworthy, despite the rumblings in my stomach as we plowed through opposing legions of whitecaps. I found myself seated beside Philip's wife, Daphne. We chatted. She was surprised to find I was from New York. Nearly all the Americans she'd met had come from California, Washington, and Oregon. I was a rarity, an easterner. I explained I was a naturalist who fancied himself a writer. "Funny," she said, "because my husband is a writer who fancies himself a naturalist. You must get to know each other." Suddenly it clicked: I had seen Philip Temple's novels, photographic books, and hiking guides in bookshops. I had shaken hands with one of New Zealand's foremost writers and landscape photographers.

We disembarked on an old wooden pier. Dark, sullen rain clouds hung low in the valley at the head of the lake, concealing mountains, waterfalls, and glaciers. A downpour was imminent. Without wasting any time, I threw on my pack and joined the others who were already beginning to march up the track.

Today's walk was laughably short—a good thing, for the rain began falling as soon as we reached the hut.

Close to Glade House rushes the Clinton River. A wide, fast-moving stream, it drains a rocky, U-shaped valley (one might call it a dry fiord). We'll hike up this valley through all of tomorrow and half of the next day. The climb will be gentle until, at the valley's head, we run into a great wall of rock. At that point we'll gain altitude quickly (legs willing) and cross a saddle at 3,800 feet. On the other side the trail descends into a warmer, wetter valley drained by the Arthur River. A trail along the bottom follows the river to the sea.

Glade House is more than a hut. Huts are small and spare. Glade House extends its roof over men's and women's bunkrooms, separate-sex bathrooms, a rustic dining area, and a cozy lounge equipped with an upright piano. The resident hutkeepers are an elderly couple who have served Milford Track hikers nearly as long as the *Tawera*.

After dinner the hutkeepers coaxed us into singing folk songs around the piano. "Waltzing Matilda" never sounded better.

12.

Pompolona Hut.

Early this morning we took to the trail as a light drizzle was falling. Gentle rain after the night's downpour was a blessing for which I was grateful.

Our guide explained that he would follow, not lead. His job was making sure that everyone got along all right and reached the day's destination. The trail was marked well enough that directions, aside from those present on a few scattered signposts, would not be needed. We were free to walk quickly or slowly, singly or in groups. This meant that I could do as I pleased: dawdle, look for birds, botanize, take photographs, and get to know my companions.

We began in dark, mossy rain forest. The morning rain fizzled shortly after we were under way, but from the foliage of beeches, moisture continued to drip on our heads. Long stretches of the trail had turned into hog wallows.

The sun remained hidden by clouds, but the fog lifted enough to let us glimpse the great height of the valley walls. Waterfalls abounded. Every hundreds yards or so, a skinny jet of runoff came flying over the rim. By lunchtime we had seen enough torrents, large and small, to equal several Niagaras.

The forest's wildlife remained concealed. In comparable woods in another country, one would search the trees for squirrels or monkeys, for deer, for the loop of a snake or the watchful eyes of a cat. Here such creatures are absent. I did, however, catch glimpses of several birds. Once a yellow-crowned parakeet, emerald green and butter yellow, landed on a limb above me. Farther along a tiny, sawed-off New Zealand wren called the rifleman ran over some boulders, and at another point I thought I glimpsed a parrot, perched on a limb. Before I could get a better look, the parrot (or whatever it was) disappeared into the forest.

Avalanches and mudslides are almost daily occurrences in the valley. Just before stopping for lunch, we picked our way through an area where an enormous load of rock and earth had recently buried the trail.

At midday, rain begn to "spit." (New Zealanders refer to

very light precipitation as spitting.) As paying guests, we were lucky to have the use of an open-faced wooden shelter. Sandwiches, fruit, and hot tea were served by a red-faced man in a checkered wool overshirt.

I had been the first of our party to reach the lunch stop. As I broke out of the bush into the clearing surrounding the shelter, two chicken-sized birds sprang out of the shadows and jogged up the trail ahead of me.

They were weka (pronounced "wekka"). A weka (*Gallirallus australis*) is a flightless rail found only in New Zealand. I had heard a great deal regarding weka (about what pests they can be, for example), but these were the first of the breed I had seen. Their profiles were henlike. Each had handsome gray stripes over the eyes, a mottled brown back, gray underparts, huge feet, and a formidable spear of a bill.

The weka were not kiwi, but they were the first of New Zealand's flightless birds I had found in the wild. This was encouraging. Perhaps kiwi were just a few steps away.

I sat on dry ground under the shelter's overhanging roof. Remaining near, a weka strutted back and forth at my feet, flicking its stubby tail. I assumed it was lobbying for a handout and made ready to give it one, but before I could act a shriek came from behind and the weka fled.

Into the frame formed by walls and roof walked a parrot. It was a monster as parrots go, nearly as big as the weka, and it had a heavy bill with an overshot upper mandible. The bird's head and torso were covered in dark-edged olive feathers.

This was a kea, the alleged sheep-killer. It wasn't alone. Soon there were four.

The keas displayed great self-assurance, strutting among the feet of the hikers, snooping for scraps, occasionally flying up to the rim of the shelter's rubbish bin to see what they had missed. For the parrots, entertaining luncheon guests was clearly nothing new.

We had been warned in Te Anau about keas. They are mischievous animals. Leave a raincoat unattended and they will divide it neatly into pieces. (Losing one's raincoat in a remote area where it rains three hundred inches a year is a serious matter.) Leave a pack unguarded and they will empty it, sampling all of the contents, eating whatever strikes their fancy, and destroying what remains. However, we were told that if we took proper precautions, the keas would prove engaging companions.

This afternoon's walk was much like the morning's. We continued pushing up the valley, parallel to the roaring Clinton River, straining for glimpses of sun and the valley rim. The lower stretches of river were clear; they are said to harbor trout, but farther up, the water, milky with glacial runoff, is sterile and fishless. Our lunchtime thespians, the keas, were nowhere to be seen.

In the morning I had walked alone, but in the afternoon I marched in the company of the two Chicagoans, Rich and Tammy. At midafternoon we reached Pompolona Hut, our shelter for the night. It looked, in Rich's words, "like a first-class hotel."

The hut was actually several huts. There was a large central building housing a dining area, a kitchen, and a drying room hot as a sauna. Next to it, uphill, connected by a stairway and sheltered walkway, were a men's bunkroom, a women's bunkroom, and spacious bathrooms equipped to handle crowds. All the structures were armored with aluminum siding, and I noticed that they were free of moss and lichen, unlike the other huts we had seen.

The cheery, gray-haired hutkeeper greeted us at the door.

Over his head, lined up along the gutter, were several keas. We exchanged pleasantries. Afterward I asked about the apparent newness of the compound.

"Yes, it's all just finished," the hutkeeper said. "The old hut was taken out by a landslide just last year. No one was inside at the time, luckily."

"Any danger of a repeat performance?" I asked. "After all this rain—"

"Lightning never strikes twice. She'll be right, mate. No worries."

Tammy asked about keas. "Do you get along with the parrots, living at Pompolona full-time?"

"Hell, no. The bloody things make trouble all the time. They're clever, cheeky little bastards. One of these"—he gestured over his shoulder—"found his way into the loo not long ago and carried a roll of paper out onto the porch. There he sat and tore the whole bloody thing into a thousand pieces, dropping each over the edge. When I came out, he flew to the roof. The bastard then had the nerve to sit there, making low chuckling sounds, while I cleaned up his mess. It was as if he had done it on purpose—just to get my goat."

"What did you do?" I asked. Keas are protected by law, but among humans they have made numerous enemies, and the regulation often goes unheeded.

"Don't be mistaken. Keas often make life difficult. I'd be a liar if I said I haven't thrown a few stones in their direction. Yet they're interesting and beautiful things, all the same, and I suppose they've as much right to the valley as we do."

I asked about kiwi.

"They live hereabouts, I reckon, but are rarely seen. You might hear one if you listen tonight, but it can't be promised." With that the hutkeeper excused himself and hurried inside.

We dumped our packs in the bunkrooms and latched the doors so the keas couldn't get them. After a snack in the dining room, I retreated to my bunk for a nap.

Tonight, after a huge meal, the hutkeeper requested our attention. The weather forecast, he said, was good. It promised a foggy morning followed by clearing and a fine afternoon. We are lucky. A *National Geographic* writer walked the track in the 1960s and ran into such rain and winds that she and her party had to cross the pass on hands and knees.

The announcements continued. We were instructed to secure the doors of bunkrooms and baths. Where keas are present, an unlatched door is an invitation to disaster. We should expect to hear keas overhead during the night. They enjoy clambering on metal roofs, the more noise the better.

"Finally," said the hutkeeper, "we are especially honored to welcome Philip Temple as a member of this group. I hope Mr. Temple won't mind me saying so, but he is one of our most distinguished authors here in New Zealand. He wrote the Shell guide to this track, and among many books he has written a novel in which the main characters are keas. Mr. Temple, in your capacity as a kea authority, might I persuade you to tell us a few things about these birds?"

Temple rose from his chair. I suspect he would have preferred to finish his dessert in peace, but he agreed good-naturedly to share what he knew.

"Keas," Philip Temple told us, "are often described as *alpine* parrots. This is true, inasmuch as they live in a mountainous region and people tend to see them when they are most visible, which is to say, out in the open, above bush line. But they are really forest birds. They feed on fruits, seeds, buds, and roots. These they find in the bush.

"When farmers began to clear the bush with axes and

fire, the keas lost much of their habitat. Other birds suffered the same fate; most declined in numbers or vanished entirely. But keas endured. Bold, inquisitive, resilient, they learned that farmers are sometimes less than tidy, that the remains of butchered sheep (entrails and things) were a nourishing source of protein.

"So keas began loitering about the killing sheds, eating the leavings. At the same time, farmers began accusing parrots of murdering sheep in their paddocks."

Several in the audience laughed, amused by the notion of keas chasing sheep.

"It *is* funny, I suppose, but the farmers were really quite serious about it. They convinced the government to put a bounty on keas, and for a hundred years they were shot on sight.

"There's little truth to it, of course. Dick Jackson, one of our best ornithologists, has shown that keas rarely if ever bother living sheep. While farmers said keas rode the backs of sheep, biting them on the neck and driving them over cliffs, Jackson found no evidence of this. Nor could he locate anyone who had actually seen a kea do the job. Eventually the government came round to the idea that this business of birds destroying livestock was much ado about nothing. Today the kea is protected legally. It's too late to help the tens of thousands that were killed, but we've acted soon enough, I hope, to rescue the species."

After the talk was over, I stepped out to listen for kiwi. The night was black. I needed my flashlight (they call them torches here) to see my feet as I shuffled up the trail. The chugging of the hut's generator, the rushing of the river, and the scraping of parrot claws on metal were the only sounds around me. The sky was deliciously vacant of airplanes.

Shivering in the cool air, I listened for an hour but heard nothing. The bush was still.

13.

Quintin Hut.

The pass has been conquered. Actually there was little to overcome. The trail climbed up and over the great wall of rock in easy switchbacks. Our only real challenge came halfway up, when the forest gave way to grassland, and suddenly, icy air poured down from above. I had been hiking in shorts and a T-shirt, but it quickly became necessary to don trousers, a thick wool sweater, and a windbreaker.

The Pompolona keas were waiting for us at the top. They had beaten us to the summit by riding an updraft at the head of the valley. Inside a hut bolted to the bedrock, hot soup was being served. I consumed a bowl hungrily, having paid dearly for the privilege.

The crown of the pass was marked by a cairn. While several of us dawdled beside it, defending our packs against inquisitive keas, the sky brightened. Swiftly the fog evaporated in the valley, and the sun emerged from the clouds.

In all directions the view was clear. Three thousand feet below, nearly straight down, we could see Quintin Hut, the day's destination. Beyond, a deep trough filled with beech and tree ferns angled away toward the north and east, vanishing eventually among faraway peaks. This was the Arthur River Valley, our corridor to the sea. Warm air drifted upward, bearing the scent of wildflowers and the voices of distant birds. Among the sounds, I recognized the staccato *ki-ki-ki* of a yellow-crowned parakeet.

We had picked a fine time to visit. Flowers covered the slopes. Two species were especially prolific: the so-called Mount Cook lily, *Ranunculus lyalli*, and the mountain daisy, *Celmisia coriacea*.

The lily is actually a buttercup. Its distinguishing features are showy white flowers as big as garden roses and dark, fleshy leaves resembling the leaves of geraniums. The mountain daisies are true daisies. Like Mount Cook lilies, they grow in clumps; these were spaced so evenly across the hillside that it looked as if someone had planted them. The blossoms appeared sturdier than those of typical daisies (ruggedness being a virtue above the bush line), but they displayed a typical daisy color-pattern—a yellow center surrounded by rays of white.

MacKinnon Pass, where the flowers grew, connects two peaks, Mount Balloon (6,079 feet) in the east and Mount Hart (5,846 feet) in the west. It was discovered in 1899 by Quintin MacKinnon, a Scotsman who pioneered the Milford Track's route up the Clinton, over the pass, and down the Arthur to the Tasman. Within months of MacKinnon's discovery, hardy tourists began arriving at Te Anau, eager to walk over the mountains to the sea.

A lure for Milford hikers, in 1899 and now, is Sutherland Falls. Third highest in the world (or so says the tourist literature), the cascade, the outflow of a lake on the flank of Mount Hart, plunges in three leaps an astonishing nineteen hundred feet to the valley floor.

From MacKinnon Pass I looked out over wilderness

stretching toward every horizon. I admire the New Zealanders for blasting no highway through these valleys to make the great waterfall "accessible." Instead they have carefully guarded its grandeur. To reach Sutherland Falls one must still travel as Quintin MacKinnon did—on foot.

This afternoon I hiked with Rich, Tammy, and the young woman from Singapore, who told me her name is Babe. We zigged and zagged steadily downward, passing through a forest of trees with trunks shaped like corkscrews, and emerged at the edge of a chasm. A narrow suspension bridge passed over a rushing stream. Rich paused. He was, he confessed, afraid of heights. But it was a long way back to Te Anau, and Rich, staring straight ahead, forced himself to cross.

At midafternoon we reached Quintin Hut. The hut-keeper, a jolly, florid man, surprised us by producing something I hadn't expected to see for days: cold beer.

I drained a can, and then another, and felt the alcohol race a bit too quickly from stomach to head. Taking a nap would have made good sense, but I was eager to see the falls. Twenty minutes later I stood enjoying a cold shower in its spray.

In the mist surrounding the falls I saw a rainbow, and in the rainbow I found an epiphany of sorts. It dawned on me that, at Sutherland Falls, dozens of miles from the nearest sheep paddock or European goldfinch, I had found the wild New Zealand I had been seeking. Kiwi, tuatara, and native frogs still eluded me; but I felt new confidence that I would find them, in time. If I failed before my departure, which was likely, I would return.

14.

Milford Sound.

I sit in an armchair, near a television (not switched on), beside a window, in a hotel.

Clawing my way out of bed this morning, after having enjoyed much of the hutkeeper's beer the night before, I felt sick. The beer alone would have left me ragged, but on top of it I had stayed out past midnight searching the bush for kiwi. Again, no luck. The only beaks and feathers I saw were attached to keas.

After another night of listening to parrot feet scrape corrugated iron, I awoke to bright sunshine and a steady breeze. A hearty breakfast put me in order—a good thing, because the day's schedule required hiking nearly fourteen miles.

I can't say when I first smelled salt air, but somewhere high in the valley the nearness of the sea became apparent.

The air warmed steadily by midmorning, turning the breezes balmy. The scent of the sea grew strong, luring tired feet onward. Here among the parakeets, keas, tree ferns, and fuchsia blossoms, it was hard to believe I would soon return to New York in the dead of winter.

For lunch we stopped at a hut called Boatshed. Inside I met a New Zealand rarity: a disagreeable native, the hutkeeper.

Keas, said this man of surly manner, were dreadful creatures. "The sooner we're rid of them the better." A woman from California asked what he did to discourage the birds from showing themselves around the cabin. She had noticed that, unlike Pompolona and Quintin, Boatshed was bereft of keas. "I'll put it this way," said the hutkeeper. "When a kea comes to Boatshed, it comes to end its life."

We hiked onward. Crossing suspension bridges over streams of transparent aquamarine, dawdling near waterfalls, bending under mossy limbs, we continued toward the track's end.

In late afternoon we emerged in sunshine on the shore of Milford Sound. A cairn marked the finish of our journey. Beyond I could see only black water and steep, forested mountains.

Now I am on the far side of the water in Milford Sound village. Tonight the THC is hosting a banquet "in our honor"—all part of the package deal. We'll celebrate our meteorological good fortune, I suppose, and reminisce about adventures on the trail. Yet I think only of Stewart Island. There I'll launch my final campaign to see a kiwi.

———

15.

Oban.

Stewart Island, the southernmost of New Zealand's three principal islands, runs a poor third to South and North islands in size. It measures roughly forty miles north to south, and twenty-five miles east to west. Most of the island's 650 square miles are wild and relatively undisturbed. The only village of note is Oban, at Halfmoon Bay. Oban is home to fishermen and the families of fishermen. At last count its population was five hundred permanent residents.

During the nineteenth century the harbors of Stewart Island served as bases for whalers and sealers from around the world. Nautical charts identified Stewart as South Island while its neighbor across the Foveaux Strait was Middle Island. But whales and seals grew scarce, most of Stewart Island's residents moved away, and the island shrank in importance.

The Maori called Stewart Island Rakiura, or Te Punga o Te Waka a Maui, depending upon which authority you consult. Tourist literature favors the former, perhaps because it is easier to spell. Rakiura means land of the glowing skies.

According to Maori legend, Rakiura was created by a godlike figure named Maui, who paddled to the South Pacific in a canoe. Maui hauled a great fish from the depths, and in time the fish became the north island, Te Ika a Maui, meaning the fish of Maui. The south island, Te Waka o Maui, was formed from Maui's canoe, and Rakiura was its anchor. In short, Maui lost a fish, a canoe, and an anchor, and the South Pacific gained New Zealand.

Stewart Island is a wild place. South of Patterson Inlet, the deep bay that cuts the island nearly in half at its latitudinal midline, there are dark, nearly impenetrable forests. Most of the island is rarely visited by humans. In the Stewart Island bush a brontosaurus could roam for years without being seen.

In 1977 ornithologists came to the island to search for a rare endemic parrot known as the kakapo. Kakapo are sometimes called owl-parrots because, like owls, they have soft feathers and thick torsos, and because they are active at night. Like kiwi, kakapo are unable to fly.

The search for kakapo on Stewart Island was urgent. It

was feared that the parrot might already be functionally extinct—functionally rather than actually, because although a few birds had been found on South Island, all were males. Only a miracle—the discovery of a willing female or, better yet, a harem of willing females or, best of all, an entire population of birds living quietly in some out-of-the-way place—could rescue the kakapo from oblivion.

Searching for kakapo is arduous work. The big birds are entirely nocturnal and live in dense bush. Strangely, the best way to locate a population is to search for tracks and bowls.

Kakapo tracks are walkways that males use to display for females. Tracks lead to bowls, basins that male kakapo dig in the soil. Every other year (sometimes more frequently, often less) males visit their bowls and "boom." Booms are low, throbbing calls that may carry for more than a mile. While booming, the male puts on a courtship display that includes bowing, raising his wings, and clenching sticks and lichens in his bill.

The team of researchers who visited Stewart Island in 1977 were successful beyond their dreams. About two hundred kakapo were discovered alive, well, and booming. At present this population is being studied. The scientists know they have to work quickly, for rats, weasels, and feral house cats abound on the island, and their interest in the birds is as lively as that of the scientists.

I inquired during my visit to the Wildlife Service office in Wellington about the possibility of visiting the area of the island where the kakapo live. The reply was a firm but friendly no. The kakapo breeding area was off-limits to all but research scientists, and even the scientists were bestowing their attentions upon the birds sparingly. It was critical that the elaborate courtship rituals of the parrots not be disturbed, and important that the area be kept clean of rubbish. Human debris might attract the kakapo's mortal enemies—cats, rats, and weasels.

Since I wouldn't see a kakapo, I would content myself with exploring the accessible parts of the island. Kiwi were alleged to abound here, even at the fringes of Oban.

Crossing the Foveaux Strait by air, I arrived on Stewart Island two days ago. We landed on an airstrip that was nothing more than a recent wound in the bush, a swath of red dirt walled in by ferns and rimu. Waiting was a taxi—the only one on the island—which hauled us down a winding unpaved road into the village.

My first act was to secure a room in the South Sea Hotel, a two-story wooden edifice ringed by sagging porches. The hotel was my kind of place—cheap, not too musty, with creaking floors, rooms with beds, no plastic, no chrome, and a bar full of locals among whom Humphrey Bogart could down a whiskey without raising an eyebrow. Across a narrow lane from the front of the hotel stood a monument to the island's war dead, a poignant reminder that Stewart Island had been linked by the politics of the old British Empire to Gallipoli and Normandy. Beyond the monument was the harbor.

On the day I arrived, Halfmoon Bay was as calm as bathwater. Cormorants congregated on rocks near the shore, soaking up solar heat with outstretched wings. At water's edge, black oystercatchers with long red beaks and pink legs stood in a huddle, looking like a convention of feathered Pinocchios, and in the surge, kelp rose and fell in pieces as thick and rubbery as automobile tires.

After leaving my luggage at the hotel, I spoke with a ranger at the Forest Service's information center. I asked about kiwi.

"They're here, all right," said the ranger. "But your chances of seeing one are poor. The little bastards are damned uncooperative."

"Could you suggest a place I might look?"

"The fern gully is probably your best bet near the village." The ranger showed me a place on a map where a ditch beside a road trailed off into the bush. "Spend time here at dusk and you might get lucky." The summer solstice was only a few days away, and, as I was quite far south, dusk meant late in the evening—about ten thirty.

All would not be lost if I failed to see a kiwi. The island offered plenty of compensations. Yesterday morning, for example, I discovered a flock of kaka. They were feeding in a grove of eucalyptus trees along the southern shore of Halfmoon Bay.

A kaka is a parrot, a close relative of the kea, to which it is a near look-alike. Both kea and kaka belong to the genus *Nestor*, named after the wise old chief of the Greeks.

The six kaka put on a fine show, caterwauling and laughing loudly, swinging from branch to branch like trapeze performers and hanging by their beaks. In the last century, Sir Walter Lawry Buller, New Zealand's Audubon, described the kaka as "sprightly, . . . eminently social, and more noisy than any other inhabitant of the woods."

I left the kaka and walked back to the hotel, thinking of Buller. One of the man's numerous claims to fame was eating a kiwi. He had met several Maori in the forest roasting a freshly killed bird; after pleasant conversation, they invited him to share their supper. The main course was kiwi. Its meat, Buller wrote afterward, "had the dark appearance of, and tasted very much like, tender beef."

Sir Walter Lawry Buller was not the first man to look

upon the kiwi as an object of gastronomic, rather than scientific, interest. The Maori ate kiwi routinely. So did early European explorers of New Zealand such as Arthur Harper and Charles Douglas. Harper preferred kiwi boiled, or in a stew. The flesh, he wrote, was "passable when one is hungry." In the New Zealand bush, during the nineteenth century, an explorer was hungry often. Douglas recounted an occasion when he made a meal of two kiwi: "Being pushed with hunger I ate the pair ... under the circumstances I would have eaten the last of the Dodos."

The kiwi I hoped to find on Stewart Island was *Apteryx australis*, the brown kiwi. (*Apteryx*, the generic name of all kiwi, means "wingless.") The brown kiwi, the first of three species eventually recognized by the scientific establishment, was described by George Shaw of the British Museum in 1813. The type specimen was a dried, gutted corpse carried to England by a Scots ship's captain named Andrew Barclay. Barclay had obtained the bird from an Australian sealer.

The next kiwi species to be described was *Apteryx owenii*, the little spotted kiwi. John Gould, a British ornithologist and illustrator, had received a package from an eccentric Australian collector named (by a parent with Dickensian flair) Frederick Strange. Inside was the dried carcass of a kiwi. It was smaller than a brown kiwi, and its feathers were marked with alternating bands of light and dark. Excited, Gould scrutinized the bird's anatomy, wrote a description, and prepared a handsome illustration. In 1848 these were published. The existence of a new type of kiwi was announced, and Gould called it *Apteryx owenii*. The bird's namesake was the zoologist Richard Owen, a man best remembered for coining the term *dinosaur*. A third species, *Apteryx haastii*, the great spotted kiwi, was discovered on South Island in 1872.

The three kiwi species suffered greatly from the arrival of man in New Zealand. Humans imported hearty appetites—their own and those of rats, cats, dogs, and weasels—as well as a Pandora's box of herbivores that set about reducing the bush to stubble. In a blink of time, the multimillion-year honeymoon kiwi and other flightless birds had been enjoying on North, South, and Stewart islands came to an end.

By the time European scientists learned of kiwi, they were already beginning to disappear. Ernst Dieffenbach, a German zoologist who carried out a biological survey of the New Zealand bush between 1839 and 1841, made a great effort to see kiwi but never managed to succeed. "In most places," he wrote in an 1843 report, "the natives told me at once that none [kiwi] were now to be found, that dogs and cats had killed them all." Worse, kiwi-skin muffs became a popular fashion in Victorian England, and like a plague, market hunters dispersed throughout the islands with dogs and guns. The slaughter of kiwi was appalling. On South Island, for example, one hunter is known to have killed and skinned more than two thousand birds.

Ernst Dieffenbach's Maori informers were not entirely correct, and London fashions changed. In impenetrable forest, on offshore islands, in remote valleys, and on the flanks of high mountains, the three kiwi species endured. Today the most abundant is the brown kiwi. Each of the three main islands has its own subspecies, and all three are maintaining substantial populations. Great spotted kiwi persist in moderate number on South Island, in the dense beech forests of the Southern Alps. Only the little spotted kiwi is in danger of immediate extinction. Little spots (as the scientists call them) live in great number on one island only—Kapiti, off the North Island coast.

New Zealand lists the little spotted kiwi as endangered, and efforts are under way to stabilize and expand its numbers.

Although the brown kiwi is said to be abundant on Stewart Island, I have yet to see one. I have walked at dawn, roamed at dusk, and twice explored the fern gully after dark. No luck. On the other hand, I have found (in addition to kaka, cormorants, and oystercatchers) red-crowned and yellow-crowned parakeets, bush pigeons, tui, and countless gulls and fantails. I also saw a white-tailed deer, the same variety of deer that roams my home woods in New York.

Virginia deer, as the whitetails are called hereabouts, were brought to Stewart Island at the turn of the century. Feeding on a smorgasbord of local flora, much of it rare, they proliferated at once. When terrestrial plants ran short, they survived by eating seaweed.

Stewart Island's whitetails are currently thriving—too well, say New Zealand wildlife authorities, who encourage "deerstalkers" to hunt them without restriction. Gunfire breaks the peace often in the bush, and several times when I have wandered far from the village, bullets have ripped through the trees disconcertingly close to where I was walking. Earlier, as I was boarding the plane that brought me to the island, I looked across the tarmac and saw a man approaching with a rifle and a suitcase. He climbed into the passenger compartment, gun by his side, and sat down beside me. In a country where crime is rare and destructive deer are rampant, such a happenstance is routine.

Earlier tonight I watched the sunset from a promontory overlooking Patterson Inlet. A few bird songs filtered out of the bush, and the sun, soft and golden, drifted toward a range of black hills in the northwest. Steadily, bluish light collected and thickened over the inlet. A raft of clouds in the south radiated an unearthly pumpkin-colored glow. By ten thirty the bush around me had become inscrutably black, but the blue of the sky was still touched by wisps of sunlight.

Tomorrow brings my final day and night on the island. The next day I cross by boat to the mainland, launching a journey that will carry me up South and North islands by rail, and across the Pacific by jet. I will arrive in New York on Christmas Eve.

Tomorrow night I will head for the fern gully after supper. I will stay there, and venture deeper into the bush if necessary, until I have seen—or at least heard the trilling of—a kiwi.

———

16.

Aboard the train to Christchurch.

Beside me sits a congenial, middle-aged man who makes his living repairing carnival equipment. He is on his way to Christchurch to visit his elderly mother. As we talk, the vast, prosperous sheep farms of Otago Province streak past our window. I am little interested. My head throbs.

The carnival mechanic is a sympathetic listener. He and I have just enjoyed a hearty laugh over the story of my final hours on Stewart Island.

In the South Sea Hotel's dining room that fateful last night, I fortified myself for kiwi hunting with a supper of roast beef, baked potato, green beans, and pumpkin. The meal was hot and filling, and I washed it down with a can of Budweiser. The American beer, the first I had seen in New Zealand, tasted sweet and sudsy after eight weeks of the local brew.

Thus fueled, I thumped upstairs to my room, grabbed a sweater and flashlight, and hurried back down to the vestibule. Night was coming on quickly.

There are times in our lives when we make great tactical blunders. At the base of the stairway in the South Sea Hotel, on the sixteenth of December, I should have continued straight ahead into the dusk gathering around the harbor, and followed a series of streets and tracks to the fern gully. Instead I detoured into the hotel's pub. My intentions were innocent. I would linger just long enough to wet my throat among the locals, then set off for the bush.

The pub, smoky and clamorous, was crowded with fishermen, an assortment of wives, girlfriends, single women, and smartly dressed mainlanders on holiday. At the near end a band played standard industrial rock and roll, but the music was almost inaudible over the din of conversation. I elbowed my way to the bar and ordered a lager.

Before the third sip I had been drawn into conversation with a young man and a young woman. "Where ya from, mate?" asked the man. He was a twentyish fellow dressed in a tattered T-shirt, shorts, and beach sandals. "Let us shout you a beer." He reached over with a pitcher and filled my glass to the top.

I explained that I was from New York, and I had come all the way to Stewart Island to look for kiwi. The woman, who had been scrutinizing me through a veil of cigarette smoke, laughed. She said that neither she nor her boyfriend had ever seen a kiwi in all their years on the island. "Best of luck. I'm afraid you're going to need it."

The man whispered something to the bartender, and a minute later a full pitcher of beer was placed before me. "Yours," said my new friends.

At it happened, my companions "shouted" me a second jug, and after that a third and a fourth. As each neared bottom, I tried to make apologies and an exit, but again and again I was halted by more talk and liquid reinforcement. The minute hand swirled around the greasy clock on the wall. My purpose and vision blurred.

Around midnight I was cajoled into joining an exodus to a destination described only as "the brown house." A dozen of us stumbled into the cool night air. Nothing was stirring on Argyle Street, Stewart Island's main thoroughfare. Quicky we put the bright lights of the hotel astern.

The journey ended at a wooden bungalow on a dark side street. For several reasons (lack of light among them) I cannot honestly report the brown house's actual color. I do recall that loud music blared from an open door as we approached, and that a diesel generator chugged noisily in a shed outside. (Oban has yet to be electrified.) The shed and the house were roughly identical in size—about fifteen or twenty feet square.

Inside, several dozen young men and women were packed tightly into a single room. They were laughing, shouting, gulping beer, and dancing with the grace of hockey players. Joining in, I took a turn on the dance floor with an inebriated Canadian woman and drank a beer thrust into my hand by my new friends. When I could take no more, I fell asleep in a chair by the door.

Hours later, I came to my senses. Around me the party

was still going strong. It was three A.M., according to my watch, and the man and woman who had brought me had disappeared. I slipped out the door and onto the street. The night was black, and I had no sense of which direction I should walk. Eventually by trial and error I found my way through the empty streets to the hotel. There I fell into bed, my kiwi hunting for the night—and the year—inauspiciously over.

In the morning I awoke, settled my account, and ran to catch the ferry. Our crossing of Foveaux Strait, in an old iron relic, was rough, and I spent most of it, as Peter Miller would put it, hanging over the rail.

My neighbor on the train to Christchurch finds this amusing.

17.

Auckland.

In a dusty corner of Auckland International Airport, I sit on a hard floor. I am not alone. The cabin crews of Air New Zealand have called a strike, and all flights are canceled. The departures terminal is packed with hot, angry people desperate to reach home for Christmas. Ticket agents are losing their manners after hours of pacifying the stranded, and angry shouts fly back and forth like bullets.

The strike is several days old. Pan Am, the only other carrier to the United States, will no longer accept names for its waiting lists. For miles around, hotels are filled to capacity.

Perhaps this latest hurdle is for the best. I'm eager to see friends and family but am sad to leave New Zealand. I have seen neither kiwi nor tuatara nor frog. But all the other creatures I have seen—the kea, the kaka, the tui—have been beautiful, or fascinating, or compelling in some way. If my departure is delayed, I will suffer the inconvenience gladly.

"Our stay in New Zealand has been too brief," Mark Twain wrote, expressing a sentiment that I suspect is typical of tourists leaving New Zealand. Only one man that I know of has ever been happy to leave this place—Charles Darwin.

After he had stepped ashore in the Bay of Islands, the future author of *Origin of Species* could hardly wait to leave New Zealand. Darwin's foul temper seems to have resulted from gloomy weather and—perhaps—a touch of Old World snobbery. Whatever their source, his ill feelings surface in *Voyage of the Beagle*:

> I believe we were all glad to leave New Zealand. It is not a pleasant place. Amongst the natives there is absent that charming simplicity which is found at Tahiti; and the greater part of the English are the very refuse of society. Neither is the country itself attractive. I look back but to one bright spot, and that is Waimate, with its Christian inhabitants.

I suspect that the father of evolutionary theory, if he were alive and in my shoes, would not sit quietly in a corner, organizing notes and tightening the lids on specimen jars. Instead, I see Darwin beating the ticket counter with a fist, bellowing outrage in polite Victorian English.

I spent my last night in the Southern Hemisphere at Peter Miller's. Peter had met me along a country road where I was dropped by a weekly "shopper's bus" originating in Auckland. During the drive back to the cabin, I reached into the rear seat, stuck a hand in my pack, and fished out a bottle of Glenfiddich.

"You shouldn't have," Peter said, "but I'm awfully glad you did."

Passing under the tree-fern fronds that interlock over Peter's driveway to form a living thatch, I felt as if I'd come home. Peter assigned me to the guest room again, and there I was reunited with a pile of excess gear he had stored in my absence.

Having spent the preceding day roaming Auckland's busy streets, I was eager to walk in the bush. When Peter crawled into his bunk for an afternoon nap, I stepped quietly outside.

I followed a track that branched off the path I had taken on my earlier visit. It led gently downslope, beneath the fern-trunk walls of the outhouse, and plunged into jungle still dripping after a morning shower. Before long I came to a shady spot beneath a totara tree. It took a moment for me to notice a little wooden man standing on a concrete pedestal where the bole flared to meet the ground.

About three feet in height, the figure was arresting. He had the long-eared, narrow-faced look of the famous Easter Island statues, and he radiated the same air of somber thoughtfulness and repose. His eyes were made of iridescent ovals of paua shell, and his ruddy complexion perfectly matched the red-brown totara bark behind him.

The concrete supporting the man, poured over a rock held in the totara's roots, was the size of a one-volume Shakespeare. In it was etched a Maori word, *Houpoto*. A little peaked roof sheltered the figure from the rains and gave cover to a sign, fixed to the tree, which said:

Tapu! Tapu!
This totara is sacred to the
memory of surveyor Monty Miller   Born
1884   Died 1973   His ashes are here
scattered. Haere Ra! Haere Ra!

I stood silently for several minutes, contemplating the shrine. Soft light diffused through the canopy, filling the air with a greenish glow. Overhead a riroriro trilled, and it sounded like a man whistling a tune that was vaguely familiar.

Peter was preparing tea when I reappeared. He smiled mischievously as I entered, and I noticed that the bottle of whiskey and two fresh glasses were waiting on the table. "Shall we?" he inquired.

We did, and we talked. During our conversation, noticing the meter that was bolted to the wall behind Peter's refrigerator, I asked about the cost of electricity. I had read that power was cheap in New Zealand because of the country's abundant hydroelectric supplies. Peter said that he consumed so little power, his chief uses being the refrigerator and an electric teakettle, that the power company charged him nothing. To prove the point, he produced a computer-printed bill from a cupboard. The amount owed, in New Zealand dollars, was zero.

Tea consisted of thick pork sausage, mashed potatoes blended with chopped parsley picked an hour earlier, shredded string beans (Peter ripped them himself in an old hand-cranked grinder), and tomato-and-onion soup. Everything tasted fresh and delicious.

Dessert—in New Zealand every meal ends with a sweet dish, since self-inflicted deprivation is not yet popular here—

consisted of vanilla ice cream, stewed rhubarb, and a deep drift of whipped cream. Like all the domestic dairy products I had sampled, the cream had a rich, mammalian taste suggestive of its bovine origins.

Coffee followed. Peter made it by brewing ground beans in an old enameled pot. After it had boiled for several minutes, he added milk and a pinch of salt, then boiled it some more. The result was unlike any coffee I've had in America, but it was strong and rich, nothing like the powdered stuff I've been drinking elsewhere.

"Dare we have another spot?" Thus began my last New Zealand evening. Peter sat on the counter, rolling and smoking a succession of cigarettes. At the table, I leaned back in an old wooden chair. The level of whiskey in the bottle sank.

Peter switched on the Philco. From Australia, BBC News brought the usual accounts of world disorder, and afterward, the announcer segued into a program of music from the thirties and forties. As a fierce downpour rattled the cabin windows, we talked over a rousing performance of "The Night They Invented Champagne."

The old songs acted as a catalyst in getting Peter to talk about "the war," by which he meant World War II. He was in England when it broke out, having sailed there to join a crew charged with bringing a newly launched ship to New Zealand. The plan was scrubbed when the Royal Navy confiscated the boat for military use, and Peter was forced to hitchhike home on a succession of other vessels.

For a short time, Peter explained, he was an employee of the United States military in New Caledonia. "What would your Mr. Reagan say about *that*?" he asked. Peter, once an active member of the New Zealand seaman's union, professed to be a communist.

Tales of wartime gave way to accounts of domestic life.

Peter mentioned his ex-wife. They didn't get on well in either of two marriages to each other, and when she died several years ago they had long been apart. He has two grown daughters of whom he speaks fondly. One lives not far from Piha, the other in Wellington.

In the morning we loaded my gear in the Morris and headed for Matheson Bay. There, in a snug house on a hill overlooking the South Pacific, we visited Peter's brother and sister-in-law. There was only enough time to have a quick lunch and enjoy a swim in the sea. The meal was a flavorsome fish salad, served cold. When the plates had been cleared, we marched down a road to the beach, Peter's brother leading the way. The trees along the road and beside the water were covered with crimson flowers, bright and thickly clustered. The blossoms were so numerous, and their color was so loud, that I found the trees gaudy. Peter called them *pohutukawa*, and his brother said that they are also known, owing to their habit of flowering in December, as New Zealand Christmas trees.

The sea was cold and refreshing. Looking north and east while standing waist-deep in the Pacific, I found it hard to believe that I had once flown over this unthinkably vast expanse of water at 30,000 feet.

10:00 P.M., *homeward bound.*

As I sat in the terminal, writing, contemplating what to do and where to do it, an announcement rang from a loudspeaker: a Pan Am flight departing immediately had a few empty seats. "Air New Zealand passengers interested in reaching Los Angeles should report to the Pan American ticket counter at once."

Needing no further urging, I grabbed my bags and ran. One seat was left. It didn't matter that I wasn't on the waiting list—the plane was ready to fly and the people on the list were in hotels. "Hurry, please," I was told.

I ran up a stairway, sped down a gangway, and stepped into the jet. Behind me a door swished closed. A minute later we were taxiing down the runway.

During my wait, I had mailed a note to Charlie Daugherty in Wellington. I thanked him for the hospitality he and Marie had shown me, and I reaffirmed my interest in returning someday, to join an expedition to an island inhabited by tuatara.

INTERLUDE

I arrived home on the twenty-third of December. The temperature was fifteen degrees Fahrenheit. The sun disappeared at four thirty in the afternoon.

A letter from Peter Miller appeared in the mailbox four months later. It brought several bits of news, including a sorrowful report of the death of his cat, Butzy. Mortality was on Peter's mind. He was worried about the future of the bush.

In writing a will, Peter had bequeathed his property to a Maori friend, figuring that the Maori were the rightful owners. But the friend caught pneumonia and died. Now Peter was preparing a new will. I was startled and flattered to read the following:

I wrote to [my brother and sister-in-law] a month ago, in which I suggested who would be a better person than Ed Kanze to take charge of this property to maintain as a memorial to our old Dad . . . an

91

inspiration which came to me during one of my many sleepless nights before old Butzy departed). . . . Until a couple of days ago, we've had a long spell of mild weather, sort of Indian summer, which allowed me to get a great deal of work done—which should be a big help to the new owner!??

SECOND TRIP

———

1.

Los Angeles Airport.

Aw, I don't care nothin' for people like that. I'd rather talk to a regular fella like you anyday."

Between flights I'm killing five hours at slick Tom Bradley International Airport in Los Angeles. My companion, a lanky Texan, is a youthful sixty-five-year-old named Charlie Stantial. We met in New York and have casually fallen in with each other, passing the hours in conversation. I've just told Charlie that the film critic Rex Reed boarded our California-bound flight ahead of us.

Charlie lives in Orange County, New York, an exurb of New York City. He is dying of cancer. According to his entertaining account, he has had part or all of nearly every internal organ removed, and twice a week he travels twenty-five miles for chemotherapy. He makes the journey by bicycle. By profession an inventor, Charlie told me he has developed a revolutionary chimney for wood-burning stoves. Creosote, a tarlike residue, accumulates in and eventually clogs conventional flues, but it cannot accumulate in the Stantial chimney. (I have sworn not to explain the details.) Charlie has enough plans and ideas to occupy him for several lifetimes.

Rather than waiting at home to die, Charlie has taken to the airways. His wife isn't with him, he said, because she has troubles of her own and refuses to budge from the house. Yesterday Charlie packed his "grip," left "the missus" to fend for herself while he's gone, and set off for New Zealand.

Charlie has recently begun a study of Stantial family history. Out of an old leather traveling bag he pulls a thin paperback book. It is a history of the Stantials, published in England. There are Stantials just about everywhere, according to the author, including dozens in New Zealand. Charlie is traveling alone and without advance notice to look them up. He has no itinerary, no firm ideas where he'll stay or go.

I told him that I've taken a month's leave so I can participate in a scientific expedition. We're bound for an island in the Cook Strait to study a rare and very unusual reptile. It's called the tuatara, and although it looks like a lizard it's actually something entirely different.

"A lizard that's not a lizard, huh? I guess that makes as much sense as hunting for Stantials," Charlie said. "Good luck to both of us!"

2.

Piha.

Peter Miller and a rental car were waiting for me at Auckland International Airport. I was lucky on both counts.

I had written Peter about my coming, but either he had not responded, or his reply and I had passed each other over the Pacific. (Even if he had received my letter, I wouldn't have dreamed he'd drive all the way from Piha to greet me.)

The car was a miracle, because an international medical convention was getting under way in Auckland, and automobiles were hard to find. In the line at the rental counter, a dozen people ahead of me were turned away.

It was good to see Peter looking well. At seventy-two he had been plagued in recent months by an assortment of ills. I asked if he was still working in the bush, clearing tracks, wielding the enormous chain saw that he used to cut timbers for bridges and boardwalks. "Yes," he said. "I'm a bit slower, but I'm still getting on."

Back at the bush, I slept well and awoke early. I feel rundown, which is not surprising, given jet lag and the Glen-fiddich I polished off last night with Peter. When my alarm rang out before first light, I thought it was the middle of the afternoon. (In fact, in New York it *was* midafternoon.)

The jet lag inflicted by flying from America to New Zealand is minor compared to the hemisphere lag—the shock of seasonal dislocation. At home it is winter; my flight was delayed in leaving New York's Kennedy International Airport by a blizzard. Here in the bush it is the heart of summer. Sunset comes late, morning arrives early, and the balmy February air, redolent of flowers, is abuzz with the mating calls of cicadas.

I took a walk with Peter at dawn to check possum traps in the upper garden. In New Zealand, Australian brush-tailed opossums introduced for the fur trade escaped, proliferated, and have become a plague upon the native flora. They are also fond of vegetables. Like many New Zealanders, Peter kills possums and feeds their flesh to his pets.

Peter has a pair of new roommates, both feline. Snowy is jet black and slender, with an engaging purr, and Joey is gray, reserved, and musclebound, a powerhouse of a cat. "Joey" is short for Joseph Stalin. Peter says that Stalin is one of his heroes, and I can't tell if he is joking.

After finding the traps empty, we continued onward with the cats padding along in our shadows. The track led us down to the lower garden. Bean vines with pink flowers twined up a fence, and corn stood six feet high, a few inches taller than Peter. From the garden we descended a path leading to the inner sanctum of the property, the grotto Peter calls Fairyland.

The bush in the ravine was as I remembered it—lush, riotous, a hundred shades of green. Only the brook had changed. Deprived of sustenance by a drought, it had wasted away to a trickle.

We returned to higher ground by climbing directly up the streambed. When Peter suggested this steep route I thought he was mad, but the mossy rocks proved less slippery than they appeared, and the ascent was made with little difficulty. Along the way I rolled stones, searching for native frogs.

Underneath I found hollows filled with water and inhabited by worms, sow bugs, and spiders. There were no signs of amphibians.

I gave up the hunt, frustrated. The native frogs, like the kiwi, continued to repel my efforts to find them. In New Zealand the only animal easily located, it seemed, was the sheep. Every patch of grass supported a few. It was not unusual to find sheep grazing within the country's largest cities.

This afternoon I drove to Piha and spent an hour watching the Tasman break over the sand. The beach was quiet, empty of people except for a surfer who was having difficulty mounting his board. Surfing enthusiasts come to Piha from throughout New Zealand and overseas to ride the waves. The trip is a dead end for some of them; Piha's current, tides, and rocks are notorious.

The centerpiece of Piha beach is a gigantic rock, about a hundred feet high, that sprawls like an animal across the sand. The seaward end, higher than the other, resembles a lion's head, thickly maned. The lower part is shaped like a lion's powerful body and haunches.

———

3.

Inglewood, 8:40 A.M.

I rose this cool, clear morning, stepped outdoors, and was rewarded with a glimpse of Mount Egmont, the only skyscraper on the enitre west coast of North Island. It is a symmetrical volcano, a perfect cone. The upper slopes at sunrise were sprinkled with snow that looked like confectioner's sugar. Tourists come from afar to view this mountain, but most are disappointed. The summit spends much time buried in cloud. I was fortunate, at least for a few seconds. Then another raft of high-altitude cotton sailed in from the Tasman, and Egmont was gone.

The Maori knew the mountain as Taranaki and considered its upper slopes tapu—the realm of fairies and spirits. As far as anyone knows, the first human to reach the summit was Ernst Dieffenbach, the zoologist, in 1840. For reasons of cold feet—both figurative and literal—Dieffenbach's Maori porters had refused to ascend above snowline.

Yesterday morning in Auckland I turned south onto Highway 1, a two-lane ribbon of "tarseal" (the local parlance for asphalt). There are no six-lane interstate highways in New Zealand, save for a few busy multilane roads connecting cities and suburbs; roads the width of Highway 1 constitute most of the long-distance thoroughfares.

The road led south through farm country. Produce stands sold vegetables and fruit along the shoulders, and greensward covered the hills and valleys to the east and west. I saw few people—in fact, sheep seemed to outnumber the people of the region by several million to one.

At Hamilton, a university town of 100,000 on the banks of the Waikato River, I veered onto Highway 3. This road wound in and out of a succession of deep valleys, crossing several hold-your-breath one-lane bridges, until it veered southward at the coast. After that, I skirted the edge of the Tasman most of the way to Inglewood. Paddocks extended to the edges of beaches and cliffs, and there were no people, houses, or towns. At several places I stopped to admire the water, which glittered electric blue under a strong sun. I have never looked upon an ocean quite so radiant—it was as if the light rose from the depths.

At five in the afternoon I stopped to refuel my car, an Australian Holden. A suitable home for the night, a motel called the Matai, appeared as soon as I drove away.

Eastbourne, 9:20 P.M.

Snug here at the Daughertys'. Outside the winds of Wellington—they are notorious—howl.

Charlie, Marie, and two-year-old Brendan welcomed me warmly. Marie has set me up in a guest room. It is comfortable and homey.

Thanks to Charlie's help in arranging it, I will participate in a two-week expedition to Stephens Island, a small, rocky island at the western opening of Cook Strait. According to estimates made by the New Zealand Wildlife Service, tens of thousands of tuatara inhabit Stephen's 370 acres—the largest single population of the world's most idiosyncratic reptile.

Before we retired for the night, Charlie delivered good news. The accommodations on Stephens Island will not be primitive. I had arrived expecting to pass fourteen nights in a tent—a tent dug into a steep slope battered by rain and wind. Instead, I find we will stay in a house with electric lights, running water, a gas cooking range, a dining room, a kitchen, and a toilet. My colleagues during the fortnight will be two women from Victoria University and a man from the Wildlife Service. There are three bedrooms in the house, so I can probably count on having a private boudoir.

There is a hitch. Rain has not fallen on the island in

several months. In the cisterns there is barely enough water to supply the lighthouse keeper and his livestock. The situation is critical, so serious that the lighthouse keeper—a man of strong will, I gather—had threatened to prevent us from landing. Charlie has worked out a compromise. We will use no water for bathing or flushing the toilet. We will recycle dishwater by using it to wash our clothing. If we must bathe, we will bathe in the sea.

———

4.

Stephens Island.

This morning at six I awoke at the home of Alison Cree and Marcus Simons. Dr. Cree is a postdoctoral fellow at the Victoria University of Wellington, a colleague of Charlie's. Tall, raven-haired, and youthful, she is a biologist who specializes in herpetology and endocrinology. Alison earned her Ph.D. by studying the ways in which the New Zealand frogs absorb and conserve water. At present she is "looking at" (her parlance) the reproductive hormones of the tuatara. She will lead our expedition to Stephens Island. Marcus, an aquatic biologist, is Alison's husband.

After downing tea and toast, we roared off in the couple's Japanese car. At Wellington International Airport we met Marta Vos, a mod, talkative undergraduate. Marta was about to depart for Blenheim, on South Island.

Alison gave Marta some money and a list of instructions. While Marta flew ahead to keep a rendezvous with a wildlife officer named Bill Cash (together they would round up the groceries needed to sustain us for two weeks), Alison and I would fetch scientific gear from the university and cross the strait on a later flight.

Several hours later we were airborne in a twin-engine propeller plane. Over the wide Cook Strait we flew, bound for the South Island village of Havelock. Alison had described the Havelock airstrip as "little more than a paddock," and her words proved apt. We bounced to a stop amid grass, electric fencing, and frightened sheep.

Bill and Marta emerged from a white station wagon with government insignia painted on the doors. Bill, a bearded man in his thirties, was the first to reach us. "G'day," he said, grabbing our gear and racing toward the car. "I'm afraid we've got to hurry."

To reach Stephens Island we would drive for two hours over rough road to a fishing village, French Pass. There we would meet a helicopter making a routine supply run to the Stephens Island lighthouse. If we were late, the pilot wouldn't mind at all. He would leave without us.

In a hamlet called Rai Valley we turned off the tarseal onto hardscrabble—the French Pass road. Until 1957, when the roadway was cut, French Pass was accessible only by sea. I could soon see why. Between the interior and the coast, the terrain, a road-builder's nightmare, comprised steep slopes, deep gullies, bays, peninsulas, and ridges.

We traced the coastline, working irregularly northward. The scenery was pretty—there were numerous turquoise bays and emerald, bush-clad islands—but the road was a washboard. My stomach, always tender in a stuffy automobile, twisted every time we swung around a hairpin bend. The car vibrated like a paint shaker. When I could bear my torment no longer, I asked Bill to stop. The action I took next was undoubtedly not the best way to make a positive impression on my colleagues.

Precisely on time we reached a wide place in the road with a view over the village. Seconds later, before we could unload our gear, a helicopter thundered out of the sky. The pilot was a gray-haired man wearing mirrored sunglasses, and he spoke in an accent I knew well. (I learned later that the pilot, whose name was Phil, was a Californian who had piloted helicopters in World War II, Korea, and Vietnam.) We were instructed to put our gear in cargo compartments in the belly of the helicopter. That accomplished, we strapped ourselves into seats, the pilot climbed in, and we were aloft.

Rattling and roaring through the air, we passed over an expanse of flat water, skimmed low over the jagged rocks and tree ferns of D'Urville Island, and started across Stephens Passage.

Ahead, beyond gray water streaked white by wind, loomed Stephens Island. It was a high-backed island, rugged and wild by the look of it, a fitting home for a Mesozoic reptile. We gained steadily on the western flank, where cliffs rose nine hundred feet straight out of the sea.

When we were near enough to the island to distinguish individual plants on the slopes, the chopper swung around a headland. We dropped straight down. It took me a second to realize that we had come to rest on a grassy landing platform.

The eastern side of the island, hidden from view on our approach, was not wild at all, but a pasture. I could see the lighthouse directly ahead, a fifty-foot whitewashed pillar of iron and glass.

Several people with hair mussed by the helicopter's rotors were waiting to greet us: Len, the lighthouse keeper, a tall, dark, hard-looking man with several days' beard on his chin; Jill, Len's longtime companion, a sturdy, ruddy-faced woman in early middle age; and two slight, white-haired women in old-fashioned cotton dresses.

After we had climbed out, Len and the pilot transacted some business while the rest of us gathered outside a low white building. We greeted each other, shouting over the noise of the helicopter, and exchanged introductions. One of the elderly women, I learned, had lived on the island as a keeper's wife during World War II.

"Did you have any excitement on Stephens during the war?" Bill asked.

"Yes, yes there *was*," said the woman. "One day I saw a submarine—not one of ours—rise out of the sea down by the Razorback. I believe it was 1943. Almost as soon as I saw it, the thing disappeared. I reported the sighting, of course—told the navy fellows that it must have been the Japanese. No one would hear of it! They thought I'd gone batty."

A look of satisfaction came across her face. "Later, a *man* saw the sub, and the authorities had the cheek to say the sighting had been *confirmed*!"

As the helicopter thundered skyward, Stephens Island's only motor vehicle—an old International tractor with a cargo box on the rear and Len at the controls—carried off our luggage and provisions. The tractor followed a dirt track, barely wide enough to accommodate its wheels, that began at the lighthouse and vanished around a bend.

Alison and Marta chatted with the elderly women and with Jill. Bill offered to find me a tuatara. "Could you?" I asked, not sure he wasn't kidding. Tuatara are nocturnal, and

I wondered how anyone could catch one in broad daylight.

In a flash Bill was gone, scurrying up the grassy slope, hurdling a wire fence, vanishing into a tangle of low trees and ferns. He reappeared a moment later, holding in his right hand a lizardlike creature about a foot and a half long. It was colored a pale green, polka-dotted with white, had an enormous head for its size, and was decorated with a row of white spines running along its nape and back—a tuatara.

The reptile—"Old Beakhead," it is sometimes called—was not the dull-witted miniature dinosaur I had expected. It was, I could see at once, lively. The tuatara had wrapped its tail around Bill's wrist and was frantically trying to claw free. Nor was it suffering its capture quietly. The tuatara was highly vocal—squawking loudly and repetitively. Most surprising of all, the animal had clear brown eyes, larger than those of a lizard of comparable size, that made it appear intelligent.

The first man to recognize the big-headed, spiny-backed "lizard" as something other than a stout iguana was John Edward Gray, a Staffordshire-born zoologist at the British Museum. In 1831 Gray examined a reptile skull from the Pacific that had recently found its way into the museum's collection. The skull was vaguely similar to the skull of a lizard, but the jaws were attached to the rest of the bones in a strange way, and the front teeth, also extraordinary, were long (lizard teeth are generally tiny) and wedge-shaped. The provenance of the unusual skull was New Zealand.

Gray concluded that the bones belonged to an Agamid lizard (the grouping that includes iguanas) but felt that it was different enough to be placed in a new genus, which he called *Sphaenodon*, meaning "wedge-tooth."

In 1840 several new tuatara specimens appeared at the museum with flesh and skeletons intact. These struck Gray as belonging to an undescribed species rather than as what they were—complete specimens of the animal whose skull he had described nine years earlier. So he named the tuatara again, this time *Hatteria*.

The tuatara now had three names. (The first, tuatara, was Maori for "spiny-backed lizard.") Soon it would acquire a fourth. In 1845 Richard Owen, the English zoologist who three years later had the little spotted kiwi named in his honor, published a paper in the *Transactions of the Geological Society of London*. In it he pointed out that the tuatara's skeleton was almost identical to the bones of ancient reptiles he had found in African fossil-beds. Owen concluded that the tuatara deserved still another name, and proposed *Rhynchocephalus*, meaning "beak-head." Owen had noted that the tuatara's oversized front teeth projected from the forward part of the skull in a manner that was distinctly birdlike.

Some years afterward Albert Gunther, a young colleague of Gray's at the British Museum, took a fresh look at *Hatteria*. Using the zoological equivalent of a fine-toothed comb, he studied the reptile's puzzling anatomical features. He eventually published his findings, and they startled scientists around the world.

Gunther noted that tuatara vertebrae were concave on both sides, rather than on one, as in other reptiles. This sort of backbone was typical of fish and certain fossil reptiles, not contemporary lizards. Gunther also found the tuatara skull similar to the fossilized crania described by Owen—there was no doubt it differed markedly from those of every other living reptile. And there was more: Gunther found enough interest in tuatara anatomy, in fact, to fill thirty-four pages (not counting illustrations) of the *Philosophical Transactions of the Royal Society of London*.

Gunther's paper makes for dry reading. But tucked discreetly away in its comprehensive survey of tuatara features is an anatomical peculiarity of particular interest. A male tuatara has no penis—not even one.

Reptiles—snakes, lizards, crocodilians, turtles—are famous (among zoologists) for the extravagance of their male copulatory organs. A male snake, for example, carries inverted within his cloaca a pair of impressive sexual organs known as hemipenes. Each hemipene is covered with soft spikes, each is forked, and because there are two, snakes can mate from either side. To form a clear picture of ophidian sexual hardware, imagine a pair of French ticklers tied together at the base— times two.

There are benefits to having a penis or penises, and internal fertilization is one of them. Sperm can find its way to eggs efficiently, without running a gauntlet of environmental hazards. A few fish (guppies, for example) and a single amphibian (the tailed frog of northwestern North America) sport penislike organs, but by and large the development and full flowering of penises must be credited to the modern reptiles.

In the end Gunther concluded that tuatara were not lizards at all but belonged to an order all their own. (In taxonomy, the order is the level of classification that differentiates turtles from crocodiles, rabbits from rodents, and fleas from houseflies.) Never at a loss for names, like any good taxonomist, Gunther proposed the new order to be called Rhynchocephalia, meaning the beak-heads. (This designation has since been replaced by Sphenodontida.)

The tuatara is a singular beast. Ancient fossils of virtual tuatara look-alikes have been found on every continent, but a single living relation has yet to turn up (see Epilogue). The earliest beak-head fossils are more than 200 million years old—in other words, they date to an era before the rise of the dinosaurs. The most recent tuatara kin died out about 65 million years ago, around the same time the dinosaurs perished. Only in New Zealand has a template of DNA persisted to keep the beak-heads alive.

Among reptiles the tuatara is what the egg-laying platypus and echidnas are among mammals—a sort of living fossil, a primitive form which, through accident, miracle, and adaptation, has managed to find a place in the modern world. Such creatures are often called, inaccurately but with good intention, living dinosaurs.

We know that dinosaurs no longer exist. That is why zoologists of every specialty struggle to get their hands on tuatara. For the anatomist, the behaviorist, the endocrinologist, the geneticist, the tuatara is a living, breathing Mesozoic reptile—or at least a fair approximation.

For *Sphenodon punctatus*, zoological celebrity has had its drawbacks. In the pursuit of human enlightenment, tuatara have been weighed, measured, dissected, bled, mutilated, painted, prodded, and videotaped. They have had thermometers poked into their rectums, have been flung into the sea to see if they can swim, and have been tricked into copulating with rubber dolls.

Few animals on earth have been as intensively studied as the tuatara, yet basic features of their lives remain incompletely understood. How often do they mate? What conditions are required for their eggs to develop? How long do they live? (The Maori claimed that tuatara live hundreds of years. There is no evidence to prove or disprove this.) And why are there so many tuatara on Stephens Island—*nearly one every square meter*, according to Don Newman—when on other, more pristine islands, tuatara are scarce.

Our job for the next two weeks is to collect blood samples from tuatara, and to monitor, around the clock, the temperature and moisture conditions within tuatara nests. The blood we collect will be frozen and brought back to the university. It will be analyzed by Alison, who is keeping track of the rising and falling concentrations of hormones in the blood of females. By plotting the fluctuations of the steroids involved in egg production and breeding, she hopes to learn about tuatara reproduction.

The information on nest conditions will be relayed to Dr. Michael Thompson, an Australian scientist who alternates with Alison on the Stephens Island visits. Mike is well on his way to a startling discovery: tuatara eggs develop far more successfully in sunny sheep paddocks than they do in undisturbed bush.

5.

Stephens Island.

"It's another rotten day in paradise," Alison said matter-of-factly, gazing out a picture window during breakfast. "Fine weather is never welcome on Stephens. It keeps the tuatara in their burrows."

The sky was a flawless blue. The sea sparkled with sunshine, and a cool breeze drifted through the house's window screens.

Alison led Marta and me on a tour of the paddocks and bush where we'll work. We began on the dirt track that passes the research station. Instead of walking to the left toward the lighthouse, we turned to the right. The lane brought us around a bend to a gate. On the far side, in a paddock separated from the others by a strong fence, stood three bulls.

At the edge of the lane the land fell away steeply, and several hundred feet downslope it vanished completely in a high cliff. In the area between the lane and the cliff, sheep browsed among scattered tufts of parched grass. The paddock, as a result of drought and overgrazing, had become a moonscape of crumbling rock and orange-brown dust.

Near the gate, a stone's toss downslope from the lane, was a low wooden building with a red roof. "This is the Palace," Alison said. The Palace was a former naval station, active on the island until the 1950s. The name was a legacy of military men fond of irony—a palace the Palace was not.

A series of concrete tanks at one end of the building were connected to its gutters by pipes. These were cisterns, Alison said, used by Len to water his flock. A similar tank on the hill behind our house supplied our faucets and toilet.

Higher up above the track the slopes were gentler, still quite steep but moderate enough to support a thick growth of grasses. One thing was odd: the ground was riddled with holes. I asked Alison about them.

"They're animal burrows," she said, "excavated, probably, by petrels and shearwaters. A few may have been dug by tuatara, which also create burrows." On the island, nesting seabirds outnumber tuatara by ten or twenty to one.

"Is there a way to tell tuatara burrows from the nesting burrows of birds?"

"Not really," Alison said. "A hole created by a bird isn't necessarily occupied by a bird. Tuatara are not above appropriating burrows by force. They will, in other cases, move in uninvited with an accommodating landlady and share her compact space. Tuatara also dig their own burrows. So to determine who lives in which hole, the only practical method is to visit a set of burrows at nightfall. If you are lucky, you may catch the tuatara and the birds as they emerge."

Toward the lighthouse, the upper slopes gave way to a narrow, bush-covered plateau. Here we scaled a barbed-wire fence and, hunched over, walked beneath the crowns of trees hardly taller than ourselves. This area was known as the Keeper's Bush. Alison explained that lighthouse workers had protected it with fencing in the nineteenth century when livestock were first put ashore. Only two other areas of the island's original forest survive: the Ruston Bush, bounded on one side by the upper edge of the bull paddock, and the Frogbank Bush, which sprawls across the island's summit. Each is protected from the lighthouse keeper's sheep by wire fence.

The Keeper's Bush was unlike any other I had seen in New Zealand. It was a weird place of light and shadow, of twisted trees growing out of ashen soil as dry and fine as baking flour. Along the footpaths, weeds grew in profusion. Several were familiar, including wandering jew, which I knew as an American houseplant. To the sides of the paths, beneath the trees, were clumps of thirsty-looking ferns and leafy shrubs Alison identified as nettle.

The nettle, I had read, was called *ongaonga* by the Maori. Like the nettles of America and Europe, to which it is closely related, the New Zealand tree nettle (*Urtica ferox*) bristles with stinging hairs. So numerous are the hairs, in fact, and so potent is their venom, that animals and people occasionally die from touching them. In 1961 a hiker in the Hawke Bay region of North Island died after blundering into nettle. In 1944 three horses cantered into a tangle of nettle not far from Wellington; the horses died. Even in a mild case, the stings can inflict great pain and disrupt a victim's muscular coordination for several days. Alison warned Marta and me to be wary of nettle during our work in the bush at night.

Today, a long day of work began with a briefing. At the breakfast table, Alison filled us in on the history and goals of the nesting study. Mike, she said, visited the island in the spring, when the female tuatara were burying eggs. He watched where clutches of eggs were placed, and marked the locations with stakes. Later, carefully digging into the nests, he fitted each of them with three electronic probes—one centered in the egg cluster, one placed at the fringe, and a third tucked in the soil nearby (to keep the other two honest). Every couple of weeks, give or take a few days, a scientist (generally Mike, Alison, or Charlie) and a few volunteers would return to the island to monitor the probes. Readings were taken, laboriously, with a device called a microvoltmeter.

The nests were divided into two groups, and each group had to be checked every four hours for a day. Alison explained that we would take turns on the shifts, measuring the probes of the first group one day, those of the second the day after. When that was completed, we would devote the middle ten days of our island fortnight to Alison's project—catching marked tuatara, taking blood samples from them, and measuring their sizes and weights. Finally, before flying back to the mainland, we would return to the nests and take readings from them again.

Today, Alison completed two nest-circuits with Marta and me to be sure that we could carry out the procedures single-handedly. We connected wires, three for each probe, one probe at a time, to the appropriate poles on the meter, took measurements, and recorded the results on a clipboard. The hours passed slowly.

Collecting data is the least glamorous part of science, even here on breezy, sun-drenched Stephens Island. The nest rounds were tests of patience. Monotony was unavoidable, because for our research to be thorough, a vast amount of raw data had to be harvested and sifted. In the process, erroneous facts and false explanations would be winnowed away, leaving the germs of truth. Hauling in the wheat of knowledge with the chaff—our job—was a mind-numbing chore.

In achieving distinction as a scientist, it is necessary to have a good mind and—equally important—an almost unlimited capacity to endure tedium. After spending a day with Alison checking nests in the paddocks, I found myself admiring her less for her intelligence—which was keen and facile—than for her stamina in putting up with drudgery. The scenery on the island was stunning, and the tuatara a fascinating creature, but playing with wires and dials hour after hour was enough to drive the nonscientist mad.

On the second circuit, as we approached one of the last nests, a shocking scene unfolded. A bull, a medium-sized monster named Whitey, had been let out of the paddock early in the morning and now was thundering down the lane. Len had planned to coax him to the helicopter pad, where he would be shot, butchered, and hauled off by helicopter. (The carcass was owed to a South Island sheepshearer, in payment for a recent shearing of the mob.) Something had gone wrong. Whitey was trying to return to the bull paddock.

When the bull reached the gate, Alison, Marta, and I were crouched beside the microvoltmeter a stone's throw away. Whitey stumbled to a halt, bellowing loudly. On the far side of the fence, the herd's dominant bull, a one-ton behemoth named Zak, roared in harmony. His protests rose in volume and vehemence as Len, Bill Cash, the sheepshearer, and two other men appeared around the bend. Len's face was flushed with anger. In his hands was a bolt-action rifle big enough to kill an elephant.

The men ran ahead, positioning themselves downslope from the track. The bull's best avenue of escape was blocked. (There would have been no point in shooting Whitey downslope, for his carcass would be too heavy to drag uphill.) Len advanced.

As we watched in horror, Whitey butted the gate. He nuzzled the latch, trying to dislodge it, failed, and spun in a pirouette remarkably nimble for an animal so large. He was cornered and knew it. His nostrils flared, pouring mucus. In his eyes I could see terror and hopelessness.

"He's not going to shoot him right here, is he?" Marta asked.

Whitey lowered his head, swung it from side to side, and gave off a wail so hideous it raised goosebumps on my back. Len aimed and fired. *Crack!* The bull fell onto his foreknees, blood spurting in a foot-long stream from his left temple. A few seconds later, his power gone, he tumbled onto his side with a great dull thud. He was lying there, kicking and shivering and bleeding, when the sheepshearer ran in. With a long knife he reached around and slit Whitey's throat from side to side. A huge dark hole fell open. Gallons of vivid red blood rushed out like water from a fire hose. After a minute of twitching, Whitey was still.

An arm's length away, separated from the gore by a fence looking increasingly flimsy, was Zak. He went berserk, battering the gate with his enormous head again and again, and when that failed to open, he rammed the fence, rattling the wire and bending the posts. On and on he thundered until, a half hour later, his frenzy subsided to a glower.

Considering that our second circuit of tuatara nests lay entirely within Zak's paddock, gathering data might prove less monotonous than I had anticipated. Whitey's death had left his comrade in a foul mood.

Tonight, Marta volunteered to tackle the seven P.M. round of nest work on her own. This left me free to join Alison and Bill for a few hours of tuatara hunting.

We set off from the house just after sundown. Like Alison and Bill, I wore a headlamp powered by a miniature automotive battery that I carried in a backpack. Several collecting bags were tucked under my belt, and my pockets were filled with fluorescent tags. Alison had given me the tags to mark places where I captured tuatara.

It didn't take long to find the first tuatara. As we stepped out the pantry door onto a concrete walkway behind the house, a tuatara lay in our path. A letter and a number were marked on each of the animal's flanks.

Alison reached down casually and picked the tuatara up. To my surprise it didn't try to run, kick, or claw. It was dark, wrinkled, and shrunken. A heavy frame and the big spines along its back identified it as a male.

"Meet A-37," Alison said. "He lives in the gully behind the house. He's an older fellow, I think, and you'll see a good bit more of him by the time we're through." I asked about his appearance; he looked as if he were wasting away. Alison thought the gauntness might be a function of age but might also be related to the drought. Tuatara lose water at a fairly rapid rate and must drink to survive. It hadn't rained in months.

Alison explained that each tuatara in her study group was

marked with a letter and number. The letter identified the original captor—"A" was for Alison—and the numbers, starting with the first tuatara a researcher captured, began at "1."

I asked about molting. Tuatara shed their skin like other reptiles. This one was in the process of losing his, and I wondered if Alison had a way of identifying the animal after his molt was complete.

"In addition to marking the flanks, we clip a few toes," Alison said. "The severed portions do not grow back, and since no two animals have the same sequence of missing toes (at most, one toe is clipped per foot), any observer with a chart of our toe-clip patterns can identify individual tuatara. Bill Dawbin, a scientist who taught in Wellington for many years, began toe-clipping tuatara on Stephens Island in 1949. Between 1949 and 1955 he marked nearly a thousand. A good many of Dawbin's tuatara are alive and well today."

After A-37 had been lowered tenderly into a collecting bag, we were under way once more.

"Ed, why don't you search near the Keeper's Bush. Bill, how about taking the gully and the paddock by the house. I'll take the Palace spur."

We dispersed. It was a windy night, cool, dark, and moonless. The visible world was entirely contained within the narrow beam of my headlamp.

Huffing and puffing up the steep slope behind the house, I soon realized I'd better slow my pace. Tuatara were scurrying off everywhere I aimed my beam. They moved jerkily, first throwing one side of the body forward, then the other. A scientist once studied this motion and discovered that the only other four-legged animal that runs similarly is the platypus.

I advanced carefully. A few animals, big males with crests unfurled like dorsal fins, held their ground even when I walked close enough to touch them. Others fled instantly into burrows. The latter were mostly females. At a distance females could be distinguished by their slender bodies, inconspicuous spines, and delicate heads.

Every few feet I came to another tuatara, and another. It was astounding that this island could sustain such an overwhelming number of these animals on only 370 acres.

*T*uatara eat mostly invertebrate animals, such as cricket-like wetas and sow bugs; they also occasionally devour other tuatara and seabirds. For the island to support so many tuatara, it must hold an unusually large population of prey animals. According to ecological principle, a massive source of sustenance—plants, ultimately—must also be present to feed the tuatara's food. And the plants themselves must have nourishment.

The driving force of the Stephens Island ecosystem is guano. Petrels and shearwaters defecate here in spectacular quantity. Their guano nourishes vegetation, the plants nourish small animals, and the small animals nourish larger animals. At the top of the food chain, Old Beakhead sits like a king, awaiting the next insect, earthworm, seabird chick, or young tuatara to pass before his toothy mouth.

Tuatara inhabit Stephens Island in great number also because, as reptiles, they require a modest amount of food. Energy requirements are far lower for a tuatara than for a warm-blooded animal of comparable size; the tuatara wastes no calories in generating body heat. Tuatara live fairly passive lives (further conserving energy) and thrive at lower temperatures than any other reptile.

A staple food of the Stephens Island tuatara is a wingless

cousin of the grasshopper called the giant weta. The giant weta is an endangered species (actually there are several species, but just how many remains to be resolved); it was common on the mainland until introduced predators eliminated it. Now its range is mostly limited to predator-free islands. A tuatara eating a weta is an irony—one endangered species feeding upon another.

Among New Zealand's coastal islands, dozens are home to colonies of seabirds and invertebrates, yet none possesses a density of tuatara to match Stephens's. Something is clearly special about Stephens Island, but the nature of that specialty has long remained a mystery.

At last, someone—Mike Thompson—seems close to a solution. By collecting tuatara eggs and incubating them under a variety of conditions at the university, he has demonstrated that they will not hatch if kept at temperatures below twenty degrees Celsius (about sixty-eight degrees Fahrenheit). Astonishingly, probes buried in soil in the Keeper's Bush on Stephens Island have shown that the ground temperature there never reaches the twenty-degree Celsius threshold; the soil, shaded throughout the day, is always cool. Mike suspects that tuatara eggs buried under trees cannot develop because the soil is never warm enough to incubate them. Tuatara eggs planted in sunny paddocks, if left undisturbed, always seem to flourish.

This finding must be unsettling to the Wildlife Service, which has devoted considerable funds and manpower to revegetating Stephens Island with bush. If Mike's preliminary findings prove correct, tuatara are flourishing on the island largely because of the sheep, not in spite of them, as had been long assumed. This could explain why bush-covered islands have fewer tuatara. On those, the reptiles may nest successfully only on treeless, north-facing cliffs. (In the Southern Hemisphere, slopes oriented toward the north receive direct sun.)

*E*ventually I found one of the marked animals Alison was looking for. It was a female, and I managed to catch her with a flying tackle just as she was pulling into her burrow. She struggled briefly, cackled once, then relaxed. I popped her into a bag, wrote her number on a fluorescent tag and stuck it into the ground, and returned to headquarters.

Alison and Bill had outdone me. There were five animals, all told, waiting to be processed.

Alison took the first. She showed us how to weigh a tuatara with a spring balance, and to measure its length and girth with a tailor's tape. Next, with a syringe she drew a cubic centimeter of blood out of the tuatara's tail. The animal accepted all the indignities with remarkable forbearance.

Soon it was my turn. I made out all right with the measuring tape and the scale but found the bloodletting more problematic. Alison said sympathetically that the vein in the tail was hard to find if the animal wasn't relaxed. (The same principle, I suggested, held for the emotional state of the researcher.) She showed me how to hold the "tute" behind the forelegs and swing its tail gently from side to side. This put the animal into a placid state, and the blood came easily.

After we were done with the measuring and bleeding we took the tuatara, none the worse for wear, back to their burrows. I was glad for the reflective tag I had placed near the entrance—without it I never would have found the hole among the hundreds of others. Sporting a new "E-1" on her flanks and a glob of typewriter correction fluid on her snout (this would allow us to spot her from a distance on future nights, sparing her the stress of being captured repeatedly), the tuatara hit the ground with all four legs in motion. In a moment she had vanished inside her den.

Now it is eleven P.M. I must put down my pen and, bearing microvoltmeter and clipboard, march alone into the night.

6.

Stephens Island.

Here for a week and a half, we have worked every night and slept late each morning. Constant repetition has melded us into a tuatara-processing machine. Catching, measuring, and bleeding, catching, measuring, and bleeding, we gather data with mechanized ease.

Each night we stay out until three or four A.M., then celebrate the end of our shift with cups of tea. Afterward, not long before dawn, Marta, Bill, and I creep off to bed. Alison usually remains up for another hour, sipping a second cup of tea, devouring toast, reading scientific papers. Her capacities for consuming warm fluid, hot buttered bread, and technical information keep the rest of us in awe.

Working cooperatively and sharing close quarters on an island, one gets to know one's companions well. Opportunities for socializing with others are decisively limited, so casual chat among ourselves is the only social lubricant available to keep our axles turning.

The better I get to know my companions, the better I like them.

Alison, serious and reserved on the surface, is good-hearted and warm beneath. To use her own favorite description of admirable character, she is "good value." She works hard, accepts more than her share of the chores, volunteers for the least desirable shifts on the nest circuit (those in the dead of night), and supervises and coaches the rest of us with good humor and patience.

For example, Marta, young, inexperienced, a self-described city girl, needs a bit of mothering to help her cope with the long nocturnal hours of fieldwork. Alison provides it, deftly. She is supportive, never condescending.

Bill Cash, my neighbor across the hall, is good-natured and cheerful. He bounces out of bed each day in high spirits, then spends the afternoon catching and banding Antipodes parakeets. The birds are rare, occurring naturally only on re-mote, sub-Antarctic islands, and recently they have become the target of unscrupulous collectors seeking exotic parakeets for the pet trade. The N.Z. Wildlife Service has relocated a few Antipodes parakeets to Stephens. Here, under the watchful eye of the lighthouse keeper and visiting researchers, it is hoped that the elegant, lime green birds will found a new self-sustaining population.

Bill is something of a historian. One day he gave me a guided tour of the old rusted trolley system that until recently (when helicopter service began) was the only way to get supplies and personnel onto the island. The workings were ingenious. When a boat arrived, a crane fixed to the shoreline hoisted whomever and whatever needed to be brought ashore in a wooden crate. The crane then swung around and plunked the box onto a miniature railroad car. Next, the car was winched up a steep section of track to a turntable. There it was spun like a phonograph record and launched over a few yards of level track to a second turntable.

Now the real journey began. The car was hitched to a cable originating from a diesel-powered winch high on the island. When the go-ahead was signaled to the winch operator, the cable tightened and the car began to climb. Up and up it went, ascending the steep flank of the island, until it crested the hill inside the bull paddock. At this point a horse-drawn trolley took over and pulled the car along level tracks (these ran along the route the lane follows today) to the lighthouse.

On one occasion, Bill said, the cable on the lower tramway broke while a group of sailors were coming up. The car sped out of control, seaward. All the riders but one jumped for their lives; these men sustained broken bones and a variety of flesh wounds. The car meanwhile continued to gain speed. At the end of the track it jerked to an abrupt halt, and the man who had held on was catapulted into the air. He flew like a missile for thirty feet, vanished into the ocean, and seconds later bobbed to the surface, laughing and unharmed.

Bill grew up on North Island near Mount Egmont. Like Marta, he has never traveled outside of New Zealand (Alison once visited Sydney and found it "crowded"), but he has a considerable knowledge of North American flora and fauna. He knows the scientific name of every plant and animal I ask about, despite never having been educated formally beyond high school, and is widely read in academic literature.

Marta Vos is, as she herself would readily agree, the kind of person referred to fondly as a character. She is nervous, talks a good deal, and has introduced me to a wealth of New Zealand slang. She is completing her third year "at Varsity" (undergraduate work), manages to see a "wee bit" of everything, and is forever going off "to look for wee bits of pink string." The string is part of a student research project. Marta is fitting tuatara with spools of pink thread, attaching the free ends of the strings to stakes at release sites, and letting the tuatara go far from their burrows. By observing the thread over successive days, she is able to record her tuatara's movements, homeward or otherwise.

During our first hours together, I found Marta's chatter mildly annoying. Now, knowing her better, I find her communicative rather than garrulous. She has a lively wit, works hard in the field, and is forever making tea, baking pikelets, or performing some other kindness around the house.

Today Marta tried to help me comprehend the game of cricket. She and Bill listen to the radio in their free time, to "tests" under way between the national teams of New Zealand and the West Indies. The broadcasters speak in an argot Marta understands, but it makes no sense to me. Marta translates, pleased by my interest.

Before arriving on the island, I was somewhat apprehensive that our two weeks of serious scientific work might prove dull and humorless. I am relieved, however, to find that humor, afield and in the laboratory, thrives on Stephens Island.

For example, the Wildlife Service stocks the research station's cupboards with nonperishable foods. Most of the stuff is, at best, uninspiring. There are army biscuits with the flavor and texture of sawdust, canned vegetables nearly old enough to be mined as coal, and sauces and condiments that are congealed and clotted. In this context, upon the face of a ketchup container an anonymous prankster wrote "T.F." in felt-tip pen. This is unofficial Wildlife Service code for *tucker-fucker*— roughly translated, "ostensibly edible but better left alone."

Several years ago a team of scientists came to the island

with an X-ray machine. Their purpose was to examine the insides of female tuatara to see if they were carrying eggs. One of the group was a reserved, rather bashful fellow whom for discretion's sake I'll call "John" or "Doc."

One night John and a woman colleague were X-raying tuatara in the lab when one of the animals wriggled out of its bag, fell to the floor, and crawled up John's leg into his trousers. Tuatara have powerful jaws and oversized incisors, and John knew it. But John was a modest man, and with a woman in the room he was reluctant to strip and pull the tuatara out before it could do him damage. Instead he ducked into a closet, while his woman companion laughed and laughed.

John's midnight adventure with tuatara inspired three poems, two of which I reproduce here. (The second, which I've omitted, is a slight revision of the original.)

To understand verse of the Stephens Island school, a bit of the lingua franca must be understood. *Lu* (often spelled *loo*) is slang for "bathroom" or "water closet." *Toot* is another spelling of *tute*—the tuatara's nickname.

Version Number One:

> *There once was a lad called John,*
> *Who liked to study Sphenodon.*
> *Measuring one day,*
> *One slipped away,*
> *Up his trousers it'd gone!*
>
> *Young John looked puzzled, real confused,*
> *Went red all over (almost blew a fuse!)*
> *What could he do?*
> *He ran to the lu . . .*
> *. . . poor tute, poor John; NOT AMUSED!*

Version Number Three was written by a man who earns his living preserving animal specimens for a museum. Entitled "Ding Dong Doc," it reads as follows:

> *It wasn't too long,*
> *Before things went wrong,*
> *Doc and a toot*
> *Created a hoot.*
>
> *Ping, pong, the toot was gone*
> *Grab, stab, in the little lab*
> *But all to no avail.*
>
> *A whistle and a song*
> *The trou' tho' long*
> *Were no barrier for a toot*
> *Over Doc's boot heading*
> *For the Dong of Doc.*

I am finding, with relief, that the tedium of collecting data day after day creates a medium in which levity thrives. (When he reads these words, "John" will surely understand.)

I've spent the last several mornings exploring a library accumulated by island residents past and present, which is housed in a shed beside the lighthouse. Under the iron roof of the shed, in a snug room shielded from the wind and the austral sun, I pieced together a history of the land underfoot.

The first Maori inhabitants of the Cook Strait region called Stephens Island Takapourewa. *Takapou* is a kind of tree, also known as *matipou*. *Rewa* means "to float." A few accounts report that the island had an older name, *Ti-Tapu*. *Tapu* may refer to tuatara, which the Maori considered bad omens when they were seen.

No one knows if Takapourewa was ever inhabited by the Maori. Compelling proof of settlement is lacking, although a mysterious stone wall stretches across a hillside on top of the island. The wall is very old and covered with lichens. Local legend holds that the stones conceal the burial place of three murdered fishermen, but the wall may be the remains of an old Maori terrace.

On neighboring (and much larger) D'Urville Island, much evidence of Maori occupation has been found. There, European farmers clearing the bush blundered upon long-abandoned stone quarries. Archeologists examined these quarries and found that great quantities of a rock called argillite had been cut in them. Nearby, the argillite had been fashioned into small, hand-held adzes. Adzes made of D'Urville Island stone have been dug from archeological sites all over New Zealand.

These far-flung discoveries raise questions. Who made the adzes? Why did they decline in use after 1200 A.D? Did Maori from distant corners of the main islands paddle to D'Urville, work the quarries, chip and polish their own tools, and paddle back home with a long-term supply? Or was the island home to an adze-making industry, operated by permanent residents who specialized in quarrying, tool making, and trade? Archeologists tend to support the last-mentioned theory.

Stephens Island entered the written record on January 29, 1770. This was the day James Cook sighted it during the first of his Pacific voyages. Two months later the island loomed in Cook's view again, confirming that he had circumnavigated South Island. Cook named the landmark for Philip Stephens, a former admiralty secretary of the Royal Navy.

For a century Stephens Island and its tuatara were largely

ignored. Too small and rocky to be valuable as farmland, too challenging to land on, Stephens Island was of minor importance, except to navigators seeking the western entrance of Cook Strait. But as European settlement in New Zealand expanded, the treacherous channels around the island became shipping lanes. Suddenly Stephens gained attention as the perfect site for a lighthouse.

In 1890 plans to put a light on the island were drawn. The government allocated funds, and the components of a lighthouse were ordered from manufacturers in Auckland and abroad.

The first work party arrived on Stephens Island in 1892, and in December of that year the *Duke of Devonshire* arrived from Edinburgh bearing a massive "lantern"—the complex mechanism of lenses and prisms (ground in France) that would sit atop the lighthouse and magnify its beam.

Hauling the lantern, and the cumbersome pieces of iron tower needed to support it, up the island's cliffs were daunting tasks. The engineers built winches and powered them with draft horses. After weeks of hard work, the job was done.

The year 1894 brought three great events. On January 29, six circular wicks burst into flame, and the Stephens Island lighthouse projected its first beam into the strait. Revolving around the wicks, the lantern produced a double flash every thirty seconds (it still does) and concentrated the light so that it could be seen thirty-two miles at sea. Paraffin (kerosene) fueled the flame, and the movement was powered by an enormous wind-up mechanism similar to that inside a grandfather clock.

During the same year, the island lost its bush. A substantial area had already been cleared to provide the lighthouse keepers with pasture for livestock. (Food delivery to island residents in those days was impracticable.) In 1894 gale winds raced across the open ground and ripped into the bush around it. Trees were torn out by their roots, others were killed by salt spray, and those that escaped destruction were burned in fires kindled by debris. By year's end, most of the island's tree cover was gone.

The third great event of 1894 was the discovery and almost simultaneous extinction of the Stephens Island wren.

The tiny bird, a species found only on the island, was observed by the lighthouse keeper, a Mr. Lyall. He described its movements as mouselike and reported, "They do not fly at all." If Lyall's account was accurate, the Stephens Island wren was the world's only flightless songbird.

We will never know with certainty whether or not the wren could fly. Lyall's cat, aided by its feline relations, killed every one of the birds before further observations could be made. Fifteen preserved corpses of the wrens were shipped to the British Museum in London. They are all that remains of the Stephens Island wren.

Xenicus lyalli, as scientists named the bird posthumously, was a compact, short-tailed creature, a close relation of the New Zealand wren called the rifleman. Brown above, yellowish below, the extinct wren had a soft plumage, and its wings were abbreviated. Nothing about its anatomy proves, or disproves, Lyall's suspicion of the wren's flightlessness.

The cats, given a modicum of foresight, would have gladly resurrected the Stephens Island wren. In 1895, the Marine Department announced a bounty of sixpence on each cat's head. Hunters were lured from French Pass and D'Urville Island. Shotguns and ammunition were provided free of charge.

By 1910, seven hundred cats had been destroyed. To speed things up, the bounty was raised to two shillings sixpence in

1912 and doubled seven years later. Targets grew scarce. In 1921 only twelve cats were killed. By 1924 the descendants of the wren-killers were almost exterminated.

As cats declined in number, hawks were declared the island's chief villains. The switch requires explanation.

After Albert Gunther made the tuatara's unusual lineage known, its fame as a zoological oddity spread swiftly. Zoos around the world hurried to add tuatara to their reptile houses, and collectors—men with bags and bottles—began to appear on Stephens Island in droves. Soon the tuatara, once numerous, were in danger of vanishing.

Freshly embarrassed by the demise of the Stephens Island wren, the government was eager to act. In 1895 David, Earl of Glasgow, Governor of the Colony of New Zealand, issued an edict declaring, "the lizard known as the tuatara shall come within operation of the Animal Protection Act." This meant collectors could no longer remove animals from the island. In 1898 the regulation was broadened to forbid the collecting of eggs.

In those days, even in enlightened circles, predators were widely considered a destructive force in the environment. Hawks fed on tuatara from time to time, so it was decreed that the hawks had to go.

During 1917 and 1918, the first 1,582 harriers were gunned out of Stephens Island skies. So small is the island that most of these birds must have been vagrants from neighboring islands and the mainland; in other words, the supply was continually refreshed. In 1921, a good year for bounty hunters, 1,357 were shot in a three-month period. During February of the following year, 1,021 were killed. Gunners began to extend their interest to kingfishers, which were also considered a menace.

The slaughter was still going on in 1931. Ammunition was free and targets were numerous. Eventually, political developments in Europe gave the hawks a reprieve. The government now had more pressing uses for men, bullets, and buckshot.

In 1915 the son of a lighthouse keeper discovered tiny frogs living in a rock pile near the summit. Several were collected, and the specimens were shipped to experts on the mainland. Among scientists, great excitement arose. The frogs represented a species unknown to science.

Anatomical study showed that the Stephens Island frogs were close kin to New Zealand's single (at that time) known species of amphibian. The new frog was dubbed *Leiopelma hamiltoni*, honoring a scientist named Hamilton who had visited the island and collected specimens.

For several decades the Stephens Island frog was thought to be confined to a rocky area about eighty feet square atop the island. Scientists visited this "Frog Bank" often, but the amphibians were only occasionally found. In 1935 a *National Geographic* writer visiting Stephens noted that none of the island's residents (lighthouse workers and their families) knew of the frog's existence.

It seems incredible that men, women, and children could share a 370-acre island with a unique species of frog and not detect its presence. But the frog's invisibility is easily understood. All of the native New Zealand amphibians are silent, secretive, and so faithful to their subterranean homes in rock piles and stream banks that Maori coexisted with them for a thousand years without giving the frogs a name. (It is doubtful that the Maori knew of the frogs' existence.) The most abundant frog, which itself is rare and lives in only a few North Island forests, was not described until 1861. The third and last species to come to light, Archey's frog, entered the official zoological record in 1942—a remarkably late date for a vertebrate species from a land as thoroughly explored and settled as New Zealand.

In 1949 Stephens Island frogs were seen for the first time in seven years. Scientists rejoiced. But bigger news was to come. In 1958 a Wildlife Service officer named Brian Bell discovered a second population of "Stephens Island frogs" on Maud Island, twenty-four miles to the south and east. The Maud population proved to be far larger than that on Stephens.

Yesterday Bill Cash led Alison, Marta, and me to the Frog Bank. We turned dozens of rocks, finding underneath several common skinks—soft-skinned gray-brown lizards, six or seven inches long. We did not find a single Stephens Island frog.

The walk, despite our failure to find amphibians, was well worth the exertion. There were views of the Tasman, of the Marlborough Sounds and their labyrinthine channels, and of the dry, overgrazed pastures of D'Urville Island. To anyone standing on the summit of the island the world of telephones, televisions, and automobiles seemed blessedly distant.

My session in the library was followed by a filling lunch of cold mutton and vegetables. Afterward, Bill led us on an expedition to the sea. After a week and a half of hard physical labor and no bathing, we were beginning to avoid each other, and a plunge into water was sorely needed. It took half an hour for us to descend to the shore. We staggered down a steep tractor path until it ended at the brink of a precipice, then zigged and zagged the rest of the way downward by digging into the slope with our feet and holding onto shrubs and flax.

Enormous black boulders, worn smooth by the waves,

littered the beach. From among them rose a stench of dead fish. The ocean looked cool and inviting. Suddenly, several of the "boulders" shook, barked, and bounded into the waves. They were New Zealand fur seals.

That evening, clean, fragrant of sea-salt, dressed in our finest dishwater-scrubbed clothes, we marched down the lane to the keeper's house. Len and Jill had invited us for tea.

Red-faced, barefooted, and dressed in a white jogging suit, Len met us at the door. "Come in," he said coldly. Jill, smoking a cigarette, was more hospitable. In a bright room with a picture window that overlooked the Strait, she served us drinks—cold beer for me, wine for Bill, and soft drinks for Alison and Marta. Thick carpeting covered the floor, and on the shelves I saw books, an enormous television, a VCR, and a sophisticated stereo system. A spotting scope on a tripod stood beside the window.

Our meal was elegant. Fritters of paua and shrimp (paua is a New Zealand shellfish) came first, followed by cold won-tons, chicken spiced with ginger, beef with curry, rice, home-made french fries, stir-fried vegetables, pumpkin pie with ice cream, and "French-style" coffee. After we had finished, the table chatter was jolly and insubstantial, and Len gave Marta and me a tour of the lighthouse.

Then it was back to the paddocks. Tonight we searched for mating tuatara. Yesterday, shortly after dark, Bill had come upon an intimate scene: a big male tuatara straddling a rather uncomfortable-looking female, his tail wrapped under and around hers. Bill timed the encounter; it lasted for fifteen minutes forty-eight seconds, during which the male convulsed in six separate spasms. After the mating animals separated, Bill carried them home for Alison to examine.

About midnight, as I stood in the kitchen pouring a cup of tea, Alison screamed from the lab.

"Sperm! Sperm!" Bill had gone out and Marta, not feeling well, was asleep. I hurried into the lab. There I found Alison, stripped of her usual reserve, bursting with excitement. "Look," she commanded, pointing to the microscope. "Sperm!"

I looked. A school of tadpolelike creatures were swimming through clear fluid—sperm indeed. Alison had irrigated the cloaca of Bill's female and place the outflow on a slide. The stuff teemed with spermatozoa, proving that a male tuatara, although lacking a penis, was as virile as any lizard.

Tonight I came upon a copulating pair of tuatara in the paddock behind the house. As soon as my flashlight beam struck the animals head-on they separated, wriggled away, and escaped under a fence. Seven such pairings have been observed thus far, five of them by Bill. At mealtimes Alison, Marta, and I make sport of Bill's unusual talent.

7.

Stephens Island.

Outside, a cold southerly wind roars over the island. Our windowpanes rattle. A soaking rain has fallen steadily since midday, and now it is midnight. The drought is over.

We will return to the mainland tomorrow morning.

On the concrete walkway outside the pantry door, A-37 lies exposed, drinking in the storm. I am certain that he is enjoying the rain. Perhaps the water is saving his life.

Tuatara cannot soak up moisture through the skin of

their bellies, as a frog or salamander can, nor are they particularly adept at conserving moisture once they've obtained it. When it rains, tuatara such as A-37 must wade into puddles and temporary streams, open their mouths, and drink as humans drink. The long dry spell has left A-37 withered and frail. I am not surprised to find him draining the pools that have formed along his runway.

After several hours of rain, A-37 looks refreshed. His skin has pulled tight to his body (or he has expanded to fit his skin), and he is no longer drab. A-37 radiates the American-dollar-bill green of a young tuatara.

All the tuatara sparkle tonight. The rain has cleansed their hides of tattered skin and dust, revealing, on the flanks of each animal, hundreds of white polka-dots.

Rain soaked through my clothes during the early evening, but I kept at my work, determined to savor my last hours among the *Sphenodon*. To my surprise, a few feet from the house I caught a marked female that had escaped detection on previous nights. Alison returned to the lab with two animals, a male and a female. Bill brought back no marked tuatara but caught several pairs flagrante delicto. Marta visited her study site and gathered pink string. I offered to provide her company, something she usually sought indirectly but was hesitant to request flatly. "Ta," she said, meaning "thanks." "Please do." In an hour the job was done.

Because of the drought, we had been draining our cistern only for drinking, cooking, and washing dishes. Fresh water was too scarce to waste in the toilet. According to Len, dirty dishwater could supply the toilet, but we found there was a limit to how many times a day four people could scrub their plates and cutlery. Unfortunately the nearest patch of bush, where nature's call could have been answered discreetly, was far away.

Bill, who was always optimistic and enterprising when we needed to solve a problem, proposed that water for flushing could be carried in buckets from two abandoned cisterns behind the house. The stuff in the old tanks was unfit for drinking—both cisterns were clotted with algae and *taupata* leaves, and one was home to a decomposing petrel—but it would serve well enough for flushing the toilet. For two weeks our sanitary system operated manually with rank slop hauled indoors in buckets.

Our water for dishwashing originated from a different source, a big cylindrical cistern with a cover on the slope behind the house. A common gecko lived inside, and since he never changed position, we used him to measure the water level. Tonight, after several hours of rain, I looked inside and found that the tank was nearly full. The level inside had risen so far, in fact, that our four-legged marker was floating belly-up, almost close enough to the opening for me to fish him out.

Bad water and stinging nettles were not our only hazards. The big bull, Zak, remained angry.

There is nothing funny, until after the ordeal has been survived, about being chased by a misanthropic bull weighing in the vicinity of two thousand pounds. The day before yesterday I learned this firsthand. Zak stood on the lane beside the paddock gate. A hundred feet away, on the same side of the fence, I sat cross-legged, taking readings at a tuatara nest.

Zak roared, gaining my attention. Then, as I watched in concern, he raised one of his front hooves and brought it down with a loud thud. He repeated the action with his other foreleg, and continued to stomp, alternating legs, again and again. The blows he struck on the ground were heavy enough to send shudders through the part of my body I was most interested in saving.

The bull lowered his head, swung it from side to side,

and bellowed threateningly. Then, in deliberate steps, he began to advance.

I grabbed a piece of two-by-three brought along for self-defense and held it in my trembling hand.

The bull continued to roar and stomp, and now he began to snort. Each blast shot mucus from his nostrils. He was so close that I could smell his rank breath and see the points of his horns.

Suddenly the bull charged. I ripped the wires from the meter, grabbed the stick, sprang to my feet, and ran. Fortunately I had an advantage. Zak was fifty feet from me, while I was twenty feet from the fence. If I could hurdle the barbed wire without injuring myself, I'd be safe.

I reached the wire with just enough time to place the meter safely beyond and vault over. Zak was closing the distance fast.

Across the fence lay the Ruston Bush. I crashed ahead through stunted trees and nettles, paralleling the wire, and emerged several minutes later in an empty paddock. On the other side of the wire Zak followed me, butting the fenceposts.

Last night Alison asked me to join her on the eleven P.M. to one A.M. and three to five A.M. shifts in the bull paddock. I would have preferred to hide in bed beneath the covers, but I am here thanks to the kindness of many people, and one of them is Alison. I couldn't let her face Zak alone.

A half hour past midnight, in a distant corner of the paddock, we met Zak. It was a relief, after ninety minutes of uncertainty, to know where he was. We had been taking turns with the meter and clipboard while one of us scanned the slopes with a headlamp. The suspense had been exhausting.

Zak was not alone. With him were the heifers. (Len, in an act of thoughtfulness, had placed the females in the paddock to soothe Zak's temper.) A young rust-colored bull roamed nearby.

The animals were sprawled under a lone, twisted *ngaio*. In the vicinity of the tree were several nests. We approached the first with trepidation.

As I untangled the wires that led to the probes, Zak lumbered to his feet. Alison, holding the meter, paused. The heifers rose and walked nervously away. The young bull groaned. Suddenly Zak bolted toward us.

Alison was ahead of me as we reached the fence. As she jumped over, I looked back at our pursuer. He had halted and was tearing a mouthful of grass from the pasture.

Alison's hand was bleeding, cut across the palm by the barbed wire. She acknowledged the wound stoically, saying it was only superficial, and needled me jokingly for frightening her into retreat. I had a different view of who had been ahead of whom, but this was no time to argue.

We still had a problem. Zak and his harem were blocking access to several nests. I joined Alison across the wire, and from that position of safety we shouted, whistled, rapped on the fenceposts with sticks, and aimed our headlamps at the animals' eyes. At first our efforts had no effect. Zak spent several minutes butting and scraping the ngaio, and then engaged in a brief, half-hearted joust with the smaller bull. Eventually the heifers shuffled off and the bulls followed them.

We finished taking measurements (save for skipping a nest in the direction Zak had gone) and walked homeward. Now that we had nothing to fear, the clarity of the night caught my notice. Above, thousands of stars spread across the indigo sky, and among them I recognized the constellation Orion—standing on its head. In the distance I could hear the rush of surf, the cries of diving petrels, and the laughing of sooty shearwaters.

The second shift passed without incident.

Tomorrow we leave Stephens Island. I will return to the mainland feeling content. I haven't found a kiwi or a frog, but I've seen and held and photographed the reptilian member of New Zealand's zoological Big Three, so significant progress has been achieved.

Although I will return to New York in a few days, I hope to return to New Zealand. I am as determined as ever—somehow, somewhere—to see a frog and a kiwi.

8.

Wellington.

We almost didn't get away from Stephens Island on schedule. A gale blew in from the Tasman, bringing powerful winds that nearly prevented the helicopter from coming.

It was a memorable flight. All of us, including the pilot, wore flotation vests. The wind buffeted the helicopter as if it were a kite, but we reached French Pass without incident. At the sound of our approach, a one-room schoolhouse in the village emptied and a young woman teacher and a dozen children stood by the waterfront watching us land. We emerged to cheers and waves, as if we were astronauts returning home from the moon.

Bill, in deference to my stomach, drove Marta and me to Blenheim at an easy pace. (Alison had remained on Stephens for a third week.) Along the way we made two stops, one at

Rai Valley to buy ice cream, and another, just after getting under way, at the churning bottleneck of water that gave the village of French Pass its name.

Gazing into the white-capped aquamarine waters of the Pass, I was thankful we had traveled by chopper. Had we visited Stephens Island a century earlier, a trip through French Pass might have been unavoidable. The channel was a necessary evil on the steamer route between Wellington and Nelson, an important port on South Island.

The dangerous waters lying between D'Urville Island and the mainland were known to the Maori as Te Aumiti. Some sources say this name was an abbreviation of Te Au-miro-o-te-kawau-a-Toru, meaning "the swishing current of the cormorant Toru." The pass acquired its present name in 1827 when Dumont D'Urville, the French explorer best known for discovering the Venus de Milo, attempted to squeeze his ship *Astrolabe* through the gap. Twice *Astrolabe* struck reefs, but in the end it sailed through intact. In commemoration of that feat, the pass became "French" and the surname of its conqueror was bestowed upon the island on the western shore.

Others followed. Anthony Trollope sailed through French Pass, and so did Mark Twain. Twain was the unluckier of the two. His passenger steamer, the *Hahinapua*, ran into trouble. "The current," wrote Twain,

> tore through . . . like a millrace, and the boat darted through like a telegram. The passage was made in half a minute; then we were in a wide place where noble vast eddies swept grandly round in shoal water and I wondered what they would do with the little boat. They did to us as they pleased. They picked her up and flung her around like nothing and landed her gently on a solid smooth bottom of sand. . . . The

138

water was clear as glass, the sand on the bottom was vividly distinct and fishes seemed to be swimming about in nothing. Fishing lines were brought out but before we could bait the hooks the boat was off and away. . . .

Twain fashioned his grounding into an agreeable morning's entertainment, but not all travelers found their encounters with the channel so diverting. Mariners of the day spoke of French Pass with dread. Lives, ships, and cargoes were often lost among the rocks and unpredictable currents.

A hazard is easier to face if a reward lies beyond. From the late 1880s until 1912, northbound travelers through French Pass could count on seeing a famous dolphin on the far side.

The animal was a Risso's dolphin, an unusual species in New Zealand. Snow white, snub-nosed, and fifteen feet long, it found pleasant sport in riding the bow waves of the ships that steamed through the Pass. Northward through Admiralty Bay and out into Cook Strait, the dolphin preceded the boats, and ship's pilots began to look on it as their guide. When Pelorus Jack reached the Strait, he would swim away and wait for a Nelson-bound ship. When he found it, he would "lead" it back through the channel. Jack was named after Pelorus Sound, one of his favorite haunts.

Jack was so faithful a ship's guide that he became a celebrity. Children cherished the sight of him. So did ferry operators, for the dolphin was a boon for business.

As years passed, Pelorus Jack's admirers began to worry that someone might try to harm him. Their concern was well founded, for whaling was then a common occupation in and around New Zealand.

An American journalist got wind of the news that people in New Zealand were clamoring to have Jack protected. But he misconstrued the facts and wrote an article describing Pelorus Jack as "the only fish in the world protected by an Act of Parliament." It was an awkward situation. The New Zealand government had been praised for helping an animal it had as yet done nothing to protect.

On September 26, 1904, in a delicious twist of life imitating art, Lord Plunket, Governor of the Colony, issued an "Order in Council" proclaiming the Risso's dolphin a protected species "in the waters of Cook Strait, and the bays, sounds, and estuaries adjacent thereto."

Jack was nimble and quick, but he greeted his final ship in the spring of 1912. Afterward he vanished. Some suggested that whalers had killed him for oil and blubber, but it was more likely that Pelorus Jack had died of old age.

If Jack had risen out of the waves while Marta and I crossed the Strait, we never would have known it. The night Bill delivered us to the ferry slip was dark and cold, and a biting wind soon drove us from the deck into the cabin.

Charlie Daugherty met us at the Wellington pier. We drove Marta to her home in the suburb of Johnsonville and turned into the Daughertys' driveway in Eastbourne at one A.M. As I settled onto familiar bedsprings in the guest room, the storm rumbled into Wellington harbor. Wind and rain began to batter the roof and pound the doors and windowpanes. In the middle of the night, I awoke to hear every joint in the house groaning in chorus.

In the morning the storm still raged. Sixty-knot winds drove the rain sideways, and the radio reported all freight and ferry traffic in the Strait had been halted. The weather reminded me of a day in Wellington two years earlier, when the wind blew so hard my backpack functioned as a sail, and the only way I could make it down certain streets was to cling to the faces of buildings.

9.

Auckland.

Throughout the three-hundred-mile flight from Wellington to Auckland, I looked down upon an unbroken fabric of green. There were no clouds, no smog, no cities. Most of North Island has long been cleared of bush, but the land that was opened up has been devoted almost entirely to raising sheep and cattle, and to the growing of crops such as radiata pine, kiwifruit, and oranges. Below the airplane there were few sprawling cities and no signs of heavy industry.

In New Zealand one can find the fruits of industry— automobiles, televisions, computers, microwave ovens—but the "trees" that produced such fruit are absent. I get a strange feeling sometimes that New Zealand is the agrarian democracy Jefferson envisioned America would become—a nation of enlightened farmers, working the land in peace, cultivating their minds as assiduously as they cultivate their fields.

Talk to a farmer wetting his throat in a South Island pub, or strike up a conversation with a rumpled figure in the Auckland railway station, and you may find that he or she displays a clarity of speech, a knowledge of politics, and a general worldliness rare outside intellectual circles in America.

*H*ere at Auckland International Airport it is 7:10 P.M. The terminal is aswarm with travelers.

I am surprised I do not have a hangover. Yesterday Peter

Miller and I split the price of a bottle of Glenfiddich and, in keeping with tradition, drained it before midnight. To my surprise, I am clear-headed. Perhaps, just as my host said it would, the plunge I took in the swimming pond this morning "put me right."

Peter and I talked at length about his land. He agrees now with my position—that to be fair to his family, the bush is best passed on to one of his relations. He has acted on my idea of putting a covenant on the deed (a legal barrier to future development), and an organization called the Queen Elizabeth Trust is interested in helping him.

I am glad. For me, Peter's seven acres are New Zealand in microcosm. They provided my first taste of the North Island bush in all its vegetative exuberance, and walks along Peter's tracks have framed each of my journeys.

INTERLUDE

In the two years following my second New Zealand journey, several notable events transpired.

Zak, the Grendel of Stephens Island, was killed, divided into his component parts, and flown to the mainland.

The Stephens Island lighthouse was automated, and the lighthouse keeper was removed from his job. He was replaced by a resident warden, employed by the Department of Conservation, whose chief job is monitoring the tuatara population.

A year after my return, a heavyweight envelope with a New Zealand postmark arrived in my mailbox. The sender was "Kensington Swan, Barristers, Solicitors, and Notaries Public." Inside was a letter from B. B. Swan, introducing herself as a native of New York, married to a New Zealander.

She was writing as Peter Miller's representative. Peter, she explained, had requested that I be sent a copy of the covenant he was working out with the Queen Elizabeth Trust. She hoped I would review it.

The document was impressively thorough. Under its terms, Peter would retain ownership and free reign over the land as long as he lived. After he died, title would pass to his heirs, and to their heirs, and so on, with a long yet reasonable list of caveats. The felling of living native trees, for example, was forbidden, although subsequent owners might still cut dead timber. A new owner might even build a second single-family home on the property, as long as that home was near Peter's existing bungalow. Mining, grazing, dumping—even advertising—were banned. With advance permission of the owner, the public would be allowed to visit. I dashed off a letter to Peter giving my unqualified thumbs-up.

Eighteen months after I left New Zealand the second time, a letter arrived on a hot August day from Charlie Daugherty. Its contents were unsettling. An all-out research effort was being launched to visit each of the twenty-nine or so islands inhabited by tuatara. Experienced workers were needed to catch and measure the animals, and to collect blood samples for genetic studies. Would I like to participate in one or all of the trips? Charlie made a compelling sales pitch. This was a chance for me to visit islands that were remote and rarely visited. Unlike Stephens, they were wild places, inhabited by plants and animals rare or extinct on the mainland. Funding, Charlie explained, had been secured from several sources— the World Wildlife Fund, Victoria University, the New Zealand Department of Conservation, the San Diego Zoo. Such broad-based support came along rarely. A similar opportunity might not arise for years.

It was a tempting offer. Nevertheless, I declined. My bank balance hadn't regained equilibrium after the last trip, and I could never get the time off from my job. My position came with good pay, health benefits, and a retirement system, but its best fringe benefit was an old wood-shingled farmhouse in the center of a 4,700-acre preserve. There I lived with deer and owls and enjoyed a bigger backyard than the Rockefellers.

A friend who was soon to die of cancer was horrified when she heard that I had declined. "Write them back at once," she advised. "Go! You must do these things while you still have the time!"

A second letter from Charlie arrived in the mail. He said he was disappointed I couldn't participate, but he understood. In case my situation changed, he said he would keep positions open on the expeditions remaining, until the last had departed. These were rare opportunities, he reminded me, to step ashore on some of the world's most beautiful and inaccessible refuges. If I wanted to see primordial New Zealand, this was my chance.

I scanned the roster of trips and found myself listed as a tentative participant on two of them. The first would visit the Poor Knights Islands. From my reading, I knew that this small archipelago north of Auckland was inhabited by tuatara larger than those on other islands.

The second expedition would spend a week on Red Mercury Island, a forested wedge of rock lying off North Island's Coromandel Peninsula. I knew from an article in New Zealand's *Forest and Bird* magazine that the Red Mercury bush harbored the rare little spotted kiwi. My resolve weakened.

In December, just before Christmas, I asked my boss for an unpaid leave of absence.

On January 4 my request was formally denied.

On January 9 I submitted a letter of resignation, bought a plane ticket, and began packing.

THIRD TRIP

———

1.

In the air.

*E*leven hours ago we left Los
Angeles, and we've been airborne ever since. We arrive in New
Zealand in about an hour.

The pilot said the weather in Auckland was warm and
rainy. According to the woman at my right, a New Zealander,
North Island had an abnormally wet summer. This year, she
said, Auckland forfeited its nickname, "the City of Sails," and
became "the City of Puddles."

Sharing an armrest, we got to know each other during
the flight. She was returning from England, where she had
gone to attend her mother's funeral and visit her elderly father.

"It must be difficult," I said, "going back, then leaving
again."

"Yes," she said, "it was not an easy thing. But now I'm
looking forward to being home in New Zealand. I've lived in
Wellington for twenty years."

The woman worked as an administrator for an association of medical doctors, in Wellington. She lived beside a patch of bush and spoke of it with pride, like someone who lived near a castle.

I steered the conversation toward a favorite subject of mine. "Have you ever seen a kiwi?"

"Yes, of course. Several times."

"In the bush?"

"Well, no."

"Where, then?" She failed at first to understand what I was getting at. When it finally became clear, she was annoyed, as if I were challenging her credentials as a native. "I've seen kiwi dozens of times, actually. But, well . . . I suppose none was really in the bush. They were in zoos."

My neighbor had nothing to be ashamed of. "It's the same in the United States," I said. "The national mascot is the bald eagle, but outside wilderness lands, few non-Alaskans have ever seen one. And an eagle, which has an eight-foot wingspan and flies by day, is an awful lot easier to see than a kiwi skulking through the jungle at night." Despite my attempted diplomacy, I had unwittingly offended my companion. She put her head against the seat back and closed her eyes.

Passengers on the opposite side of the cabin gasped in delight. A full eclipse of the moon was under way.

Arriving in New Zealand and venturing again into fresh air and green countryside is an appealing prospect. I'm looking forward to the research trips and the prospect of seeing a kiwi. But I'm worried. Peter Miller has not responded to a letter in several months. The last I heard from him, he had suffered a mild stroke.

The first item on my itinerary is making my way to the bush. I hope to find Peter well, but I cannot be sure he is even alive. In his last letter, written in a wavering hand, he said he didn't expect to be "on deck" much longer.

Piha.

As I emerged from customs, Peter was waiting at the gate. He looked older, but so did I, and for a man in imperfect health who was about to turn seventy-five, he was in good strength and spirits. His doctor—"a pretty young American woman," he said with a wide smile—told him last week that he could probably "carry on in the bush for several more years."

———

2.

Sandy Bay, Waiheke Island.

"Would either of you jokers like a glass of piss?" Thus George Green greeted Peter and me as we walked up the path to his door.

After arriving on the Auckland ferry and navigating several of Waiheke Island's narrow, winding roads, we had found our way to George Green's cabin on a hill above the sea. George, when he stepped out the door, was dressed in a tattered undershirt and sun-bleached trousers. He had short gray hair and a round belly, and his face wore a look of mischief. Piss? I couldn't be sure what to make of this man. I hoped he was proffering beer.

I did know that George was a retired seaman, an old "cobber" (friend) of Peter's. The two of them had been shipmates, on and off, for fifty years. "Through thick and thin," Peter told me on the ferry, "George and I have been good mates." The two were in their twenties when they met.

During the half century that followed, Peter married and raised a family, but George remained a bachelor. For years he had lived alone on Waiheke Island, in a spacious one-story wooden house he built himself on a bluff overlooking the South Pacific.

Several New Zealanders I've met have described Waiheke as a "busy suburb of Auckland," a place of former beauty which is "not what it used to be." Downtown Auckland is only about sixteen miles away. Experience has taught me to be wary of such descriptions. A New Zealand native's idea of ruined Eden usually turns out to be an American or European's vision of paradise.

So it has proven to be. Yesterday George, Peter, and I took the grand tour of the island. Because Peter was feeling shaky and George doesn't drive, I climbed behind the wheel of the Morris.

We rumbled up and down hills and around hairpin corners. The interior of the island consisted mostly of green, dusty paddocks in which mobs of sheep grazed peacefully. Because there were no other cars outside of the village, the only obstacles to beware (I'm not accustomed to driving on the left) were stray ewes and lambs and an occasional dairy cow. The island is narrow and about ten miles long, so we were rarely out of sight of the sea.

After rounding a bend near the south end of the island, we came to an inward curve of the shoreline. A wooden sign fixed to a fencepost said the place was "Cactus Bay," a name that struck me as odd for the South Pacific. Ahead, at the edge of the road, I was startled to see a young woman hitchhiking. She was tall, handsomely proportioned, and deeply tanned. Long raven hair trailed down the back of her one-piece swimsuit. Peter and George insisted that we offer her a ride.

"Hi," the woman said, climbing in the car. "Thanks a lot. It's really getting hot out there." The diction and the accent were not antipodean.

Within a few minutes we were enjoying a good laugh. The woman's name was Vivian Berry, and she had lived most of her life within a dozen miles of my hometown. During a recent summer, one of her best friends had worked for me at the museum where I was curator. Vivian had spent the last two months hitchhiking alone through the main New Zealand islands. She said it had been "an outrageously good experience."

George persuaded Vivian to return with us to his house for tea. An hour later we were eating beefsteak, and fresh vegetables that George and Vivian picked from the garden. We sampled all of George's chief crops—tomatoes, string beans, silver-beet (a flavorsome green cooked and eaten like spinach), lettuce, and beetroot (red beet). On Waiheke the growing season lasts nearly all of the year, and a well-tended garden such as George's can be highly productive. George raises more vegetables than he can consume himself. This morning, as we set out on our drive, we stopped at the house of a young woman George had gotten to know. She had no job, no husband, and three hungry children. On the front porch George placed a box heaped with fresh vegetables.

The heart of George's bungalow was a big sunny room. It was ringed by shelves and tables, all holding nautical memorabilia. Peter gave Vivian and me a tour.

Peter showed us a pair of model ships. Each was wooden,

several feet in length, and laced with an intricate web of twine. "Our George," said Peter, "built these ships himself. Look at the rigging. It's perfect, every bit of it, just as it would be on a real ship."

Next, he showed us a set of miniature blocks-and-tackles. "These are rigged properly, too," Peter said. "It must have taken George a month to make them." George was planning to donate "the lot" to the local Sea Scouts.

Peter ended the tour by pointing to paintings of sailing ships. A dozen were framed watercolors, while others, miniatures, were brushed on the insides of seashells. "Imagine our friend being this clever," said Peter, winking. The pictures, full of billowing sails, seabirds, and white-capped seas, radiated a wild and windy veracity.

As Vivian was leaving, George insisted that she take as a gift a shell with a full-rigged ship painted inside. The evening ended with several glasses of piss—George's fine home-brewed beer.

In the morning one of George's framed watercolors, wrapped in brown paper, was resting against my pack.

———

3.

The Bush, Piha.

I've wondered since meeting Peter how he acquired the scars that cover one of his legs. Such a curiosity cannot be satisfied within the limits of good manners, so I waited for an explanation to arise on its own.

The disfigurement, I learned last night, was caused by a burn. In 1960, after a long day in the sun on a fishing boat, Peter drove home to the bush, stopping at a pub along the way. It was a chilly winter night, and when he finally reached his cabin he pulled a chair close to an electric heater, settled into it, and fell into a dead sleep.

He awakened sometime later. A bright light was shining on his face. Puzzled, he soon realized that his plastic windbreaker, his neck and face, and his hair were burning. He tried to pull off the windbreaker but it melted and stuck. His hands were burned so severely he could see the bones inside. He ran out of the house and rolled on the lawn. The wet grass extinguished the flames.

It was the middle of the night. Peter was oozing lymph all over. His mouth was dry, painfully so, and his tongue had swollen grotesquely. His first thought was to crawl into bed and wait for morning, but he worried that his tongue might swell further and block his windpipe, and he didn't like the idea of neighborhood children (every afternoon in those days, several came to visit) finding him dead in his bunk. So he sought help. Too confused to use the telephone or drive, dressed only in trousers, he staggered to the house of a neighbor. Deep blistering burns covered his chest, an ear, his neck, his face, and an entire arm and hand.

A woman responded to Peter's knocking. She screamed and refused to let him enter. (Later she apologized, explaining that his appearance, and the smell of burned flesh, had horrified her.) Her husband, better composed, drove Peter to the hospital. By the time they arrived, Peter had lost consciousness.

Two days later Peter awakened to find saline solution

and plasma trickling into his arm through tubes. His burns were allowed to heal for several days, then skin grafts were attempted. He felt little pain, although the thigh from which the transplanted skin was peeled hurt considerably. Several months later, he was back on his feet.

Peter said he still got angry each time he remembered the first words spoken to him as he regained consciousness. An ugly old nurse, as he described her, said, "That's what you get for smoking in bed!"

I'm writing now on a bench in Peter's garden. Deep in the bush, I look up at the sky and find it cobalt blue. There are no clouds. The summer sun is bright and strong, and I can feel it steaming the February chill from my bones.

In the trees, thousands of cicadas buzz. Their singing reminds me of August days during my childhood when cicadas (locusts, we called them) portended grim, imminent events— the end of summer and the resumption of schoolwork. The singing of these cicadas is a mix of tenor buzzing (each buzz grows louder and more insistent as it culminates) and bass clacking. The clacking duplicates exactly the noise one hears while passing between railroad cars. Both sounds are produced by a mouse-sized black-and-green insect with broad translucent wings. The veins in the wings resemble Victorian ironwork.

I rarely carry a notebook into the field, preferring instead to record thoughts at night after they have had a chance to ripen. Today I break precedent. Painting a word picture of an environment as lush as the bush isn't easy; I thought it might help to record impressions from time to time as I moved among the tracks.

This year the garden is nearly empty. There are only a

few tomato plants and a scattering of climbing beans. Because he hadn't counted on being alive at harvest time, Peter hadn't done much planting.

Suddenly I hear a bird's wings beat noisily overhead. A bush pigeon is passing through the top of a *rimu*, a tree that looks like a cross between a weeping willow and a spruce. The pigeon vanishes.

In the distance traffic roars along the Piha Road. It is Sunday morning, and people are going to the beach. The sound is new here: I cannot recall hearing automobiles on earlier visits. Peter said that in the last two years the flow of cars had swollen from a trickle to a torrent, especially on weekends.

A cool breeze blows from the north. I hear dozens of birds twittering softly among the trees. The only ones I can see are silver-eyes (wax-eyes, Peter calls them), compact, warbler-sized birds of drab green touched with a hint of brighter yellow. Silver circles outline their eyes.

A *tui*, the most handsome of the New Zealand honeyeaters, rattles nearby. I search for it with binoculars, hoping to spot the big black bird with its collar of lace, but do not succeed.

On the way to the swimming pond I see silver fern, a tree fern with fronds whose undersides shimmer like quicksilver; *kohekohe*, a tree with many-parted leaves, like those of ash; ti tree; a few sapling *totara*, an evergreen podocarp reminiscent of yew; ferns and lycopods creeping over the ground and crawling up trunks; lancewood; nikau palm; a climbing species of maidenhair fern, delicate as its relatives that grow in New York; and a mature totara, four feet in diameter. The big totara is weighed down with epiphytes, or perching plants, one of which serves as a sort of flowerpot for another tree. The walking track, cut deeply into the hillside, descends.

Now I sit at pond's edge. The traffic noise is lost here. Only the buzzing and clacking of the cicadas, and the faint trickling of a brook, break the stillness.

The swimming hole comes as an unexpected touch of civilization when one approaches it through the jungle. A miniature Lake Powell, it is held back by a concrete dam about twenty-five feet across and six feet high. The pool is deep—deep enough to dive into without getting hurt.

On the bench I sit within arm's reach of a round table that has no legs. Built by Peter around the trunk of a nikau, the table appears to have been impaled by the palm. Several feet beyond the palm and the table, the lawn ends and the swimming hole begins. Directly opposite, about twenty feet across the water, is a slide.

Peter built the slide from a salvaged length of corrugated "aluminium" he got from his oldest brother. He had the corrugations rolled flat by a metal smith and shaped the edges himself into ridges so smooth and true they appear machine-made. To use the slide, one must follow a track through the bush to the top, take a can of water marked "Leave Filled," pour the contents into the outlet hose of a pump, work the pump's lever back and forth until the water flows, refill the can per instructions, crank the pump a few more times, and hop aboard.

The descent is swift. At the bottom, the water is cold and refreshing. An underwater stairway leads out of the pool to a grassy terrace.

Afloat on the water I find a leggy, grasshopperlike creature—a tree *weta*. It appears to be dead, so I fish it out for a closer look. Reviving at once, the weta pricks me in the palm with one of the thorny spines covering its legs. I place it on the bench beside me and touch one of the wiry antennae.

Responding with a loud rasping sound, the insect convinces me to tease it no further.

At the pond's edge, a *mamaku* (black tree fern) is unfurling a new frond. The fresh growth, far larger than a typical fern fiddlehead, resembles the head of a string bass.

The brook below the dam gurgles slowly, and I find the sound soothing. In the bush a riroriro sings its "I will love you always" song. Earlier, at dawn, I came to the pond to bathe and saw one of these birds up close in a tree near the changing-house. Its body was wren sized and the plumage was colored battleship gray. There was nothing in the riroriro's prosaic appearance to suggest the haunting, bittersweet quality of its song.

A bath at Peter's in summertime is enjoyed al fresco. This morning, carefully following my host's instructions, I filled a bucket with hot water ladled from a pot simmering on the cookstove, mixed in cold water drained from an old brass valve above Peter's kitchen sink, carried soap and a towel, and walked to the pond. Standing on the concrete walkway below the dam, I stripped, as Peter had advised, and wet my hair by leaning into the water. Then, dousing myself with warm water from the bucket, I lathered myself from head to toe with soap and shampoo. For several minutes I stood with my eyes closed, letting the soap do its work, listening to the riroriro. When a chill began to creep over me, I patted my eyes dry, walked naked and soapy through the bush to the top of the slide, primed the pump, and raced down the cold metal into the pond.

It was a bit more work than turning on a shower but far more atmospheric.

I take a detour near the slide and climb to a clearing where there is a bench and table. Sitting, I look over a mile of jungle to the Tasman. The western horizon looks as if it were drawn with a ruler. There is little difference between placid sea and placid sky, save that the sea's blue is marginally darker than the sky's.

In the apex of a cut through the trees, I see Lion Rock with surf crashing against its base. The great stone feline is alert, head up and facing the sea, as if at any moment it might rise and bound into the waves.

I descend toward the place Peter calls Fairyland. Liverworts (primitive, nonvascular plants) creep across the path; they are thin, green, and lettucelike. In the bush the variety and abundance of liverworts and of lycopods, mosses, and ferns is astonishing.

A tui calls, its voice a pleasing jumble of gulps, whistles, and rattles. A riroriro trills, as if to reply. Although repetitive, the riroriro's song is so pure in tone and so earnest in delivery that I cannot hear enough of it.

Now I stand at the base of a monstrous rimu. A sign is nailed to the trunk: NOTICE: THIS RIMU TREE IS ON THE PROPERTY OF M. H. MILLER. Peter says the property line actually runs through the tree, in favor of his neighbor, but he has no intention of removing the sign. Long ago, when most of his neighbors were selling their big trees to sawmills, Monty Miller, Peter's father, refused to let lumberjacks set foot on his property. Peter keeps the faith.

I pick my way down into Fairyland and find it unchanged. Myriad sensations come to mind, several of them contradictory. I sit on one of Peter's well-placed handmade benches to record what I see and feel.

The grotto, with its blend of brook and jungle, is simultaneously silent, noisy (the sound of water, the cicadas), serene, and riotous (the extravagant vegetation pushing in from above, underfoot, upstream, downstream, the flanks).

The rocks, in places where the water flows directly over them, are blackened by dark algae. Elsewhere in the creek bed, a moss of extraordinary verdure covers the stones. Clumps of some shrubby wildflower—it looks like a gargantuan relation of Solomon's seal, a wild lily common in New York—encircle the pool, their serrated leaves tinged with purple. Autumn is coming. The air is cool, expectant.

I follow a narrow path downstream to a bench beside a bridge. Both are good examples of Peter Miller's handiwork. Constructed of hand-hewn timber, the bench and the bridge are ingenious in the graceful simplicity of their designs, and in the way they look as inseparable from the bush as the nikau palm and the tree fern.

Peter is a poet. But instead of marrying words to thoughts and images, as most poets do, he weds footpaths and wooden creations to landscape. The bush—his masterwork, perhaps his only work—is a *Leaves of Grass* built with hands and wheelbarrow. It is constantly growing and evolving—as Whitman's volume of poetry did during his lifetime—taking on new shapes, incorporating new ideas. Peter has plans for additional trails. There are footbridges he wants to build, and places of rare beauty, ideal for quiet contemplation, where he hopes to put benches. He works every day, year after year, driven by an inner compulsion that he cannot explain.

After crossing another bridge, I come to a ladder fashioned from lengths of dark hand-cut hardwood. I climb it and emerge, fifteen feet higher, on the rim of the gorge.

At this viewpoint, the bush around me grows riotously, and the gurgle of the stream in the gorge remains audible, but the magical essence of Fairyland has been lost. There is more sunshine here, the cicadas are noisier, and I can see fragments of the sky through gaps in the foliage. Below, I was immersed in a dank underworld—the hiding place, one could easily imagine, of fairies, water sprites, and the elusive native frogs.

I ascend quickly, pausing several times to catch my breath. The track, I observe during one rest stop, has been built with great sensitivity to the bush through which it passes. It adds to, rather than detracts from, the visual appeal of the scene. The track is narrow, no wider than it needs to be for a man or wheelbarrow to pass. Unobtrusive earthen gutters parallel the walking surface, ceramic pipes run under the junctions, and here and there additional pipes are positioned to channel heavy runoff safely into the bush.

I hear a pigeon again, its whistling wings the giveaway. Like the other birds of the bush, pigeons are often heard but infrequently seen.

A tui calls.

I sit on a bench beneath the lone, grand kauri. The trunk towers over the bush like a great doric column with no hint of taper. It is the only tree within view not encrusted with moss, fern, and epiphytes. According to Peter, this is because the kauri sheds its bark in thick plates. An ingenious defense, if that's what it is—other large trees here are burdened with hangers-on, and it is not uncommon for some of them to topple after their epiphytes absorb a heavy rain. The exfoliating gives the kauri a handsome, patchy look. A single colony of moss clings to the lower trunk; it is exactly the shape of Australia.

I look up and am blinded. The Tasman is reflecting the afternoon sun like a mirror. The sky has grown cloudy, and the water is now a brilliant silvery white.

Looking for birds, I crane my neck to scan the kauri's high branches. A flock of silver-eyes arrives and departs. I note a wash of lemon yellow that colors their crowns and napes. An English chaffinch flies into view. It reminds me of a slimmed-down female rose-breasted grosbeak, an American bird.

As I turn to leave, an Indian myna—the least appreciated and most conspicuous member of New Zealand's immigrant birds—perches in a nearby rimu. It is a dark and robin sized. Yellow patches surround its eyes like the makeup of a circus clown.

I climb upslope along the track to a point opposite the level of the kauri (about forty feet up) where branches begin to sprout from its bole. A parrot banks in for a landing. Its torso is a brilliant yellow-green, the head and a neckband are a vivid crimson, and the wings and tail are edged in blue. Chattering to itself, the bird lingers for several minutes before flying off. It is an eastern rosella, an exotic bird imported to New Zealand from Australia. Eastern rosellas were once sold as pets, and today the descendants of escaped birds thrive in bush-covered areas of North Island.

The trail leads me back into the jungle. I promptly encounter a fantail, a chickadee-sized bird that flashes its long tail again and again. The light has taken on the golden color that is peculiar to summer afternoons.

Beside the path I see a rock. It is dark, humpbacked, round in general outline, about the diameter of a dinner plate. Moss encrusts it like green hair. I turn the rock over, hoping to find a frog beneath, but instead discover a fat spider guarding white, pea-sized eggs. Already on this visit I have looked under dozens, perhaps hundreds, of similar stones. I have found no sign of a native frog.

Returning to the cabin, I find Peter putting the finishing touches on our tea. It is just like old times, save for the conspicuous absence of Glenfiddich. Peter's doctor insists he stay away from the stuff, although he suggested we could override the order and buy a bottle on the drive home from the airport.

I persuaded him to accept a compromise: we will abstain from liquor now but celebrate properly two months hence, on the eve of my departure for America.

4.

Waimamaku.

Yesterday morning I rented a car in Whangarei, a port city of 40,000. Whangarei is the only metropolis of significant size north of Auckland.

I drove west on Highway 14, heading for Dargaville, on the Tasman Coast. There I would turn north on a road leading to the Waipoa Forest, the home of ancient kauri trees, the biggest and oldest in New Zealand.

The road passed through terrain so familiar that it gave me a sense of déjà vu. All the original bush had been stripped away, laying bare a series of alleys and hills. Paddocks dotted with sheep and dairy cows stretched toward the four points of the compass; they were identical, right down to the species of grasses in the pastures and the weeds along the fences, to places I have visited in Pennsylvania, New York, and New England. On the ridgetops, trees grew—not rata, rimu, or kauri, but North American pines and poplars.

It seemed as if a grand deception had been staged for my benefit, as if someone were going to extravagant lengths to convince me I was somewhere other than in New Zealand.

As the hours passed I began to notice that the farms lacked barns. Overt signs of human presence were few and far between—I saw a farmhouse here, a farmhouse there, but great gaps loomed between them, and the hulking cowsheds and weatherbeaten outbuildings that characterize American farms were missing. Winters are mild here. Sheep ranchers and dairymen can keep their animals outside in paddocks all year. The animals rarely if ever need to be housed, and the farmer is spared the necessity of growing and storing hay and silage for winter food. As a result farming in northern North Island, relative to most places in the world, is lucrative.

My déjà vu extended even into the villages. The people I saw strolling the sidewalks and driving in automobiles appeared strangely familiar. The sensation could be unsettling. More than once I developed a feeling that dead people I had known—my grandparents, for example—were alive here in some small out-of-the-way town, pursuing a comfortable, antipodean afterlife in a sunny green heaven. I tried to banish such thoughts but they returned, around another bend, in another alien town. I found myself searching for faces that I recognized.

New Zealand, in several ways, is a looking-glass version of the world I left behind. Country roads look exactly like those back home, but cars drive on the left, rather than the right. The interior of the car I drive resembles dozens I've driven before, save that the wheel and gauges are positioned before the wrong seat. In houses, the electrical outlets are similar to those in America, yet each possesses a toggle switch to control the current, a feature not found in outlets at home. The light switches on walls look identical to those I know, except down is on and up is off. Such reversals of the expected can be troubling in bathrooms. More than once I have turned on a "cold" tap and thrust my hands into the stream, only to discover too late, feeling sudden pain, that I have twisted the wrong spigot.

In Dargaville, a tourist town that once served as an important timber port, I turned north on Highway 12. The pavement gave way to metal (gravel), the low hills became high hills, and the pines and poplars on the ridges gave way to patches of native bush. The pastures grew scruffier and more widely spaced.

After entering the Waipoa Forest, the road wound back and forth in dim light, following deep, bush-filled ravines parted by rushing streams. Looming overhead were enormous kauri, one and two hundred feet in height. The crowns of the trees were high and spreading, and they bristled with narrow gray-green leaves.

By anyone's standard, kauri are impressive trees. Even Darwin, who disliked just about everything he found in New Zealand, looked begrudgingly up to the tree he called "the great kauri pine." Kauri, he noted, were "noble" and "gigantic."

I continued northward for several miles. The forest covered about 22,000 acres, but only 6,000 acres supported mature kauri. Along the shoulder of the road I searched for a trail that would lead me to the most ancient stand of kauri in New Zealand.

In early afternoon I pulled off on a dusty shoulder. A track led into dense bush, and soon it brought me to the kauri known as Tane Mahuta, the "Lord of the Forest."

At last count the height of Tane Mahuta was one hundred seventy feet. Its girth was forty-five feet, and in area its crown was estimated to cover nearly twelve thousand square feet—about one and a half times the size of a baseball diamond. Tane Mahuta is more than a millennium old. It was growing here, no doubt, before man ever set foot in New Zealand.

Until Europeans settled New Zealand, kauri grew throughout the northern half of the north island. Then, between 1850 and 1950, nearly all the big trees were cut, hauled to mills on narrow-gauge railways, and sawn into boards. Kauri, strong but easily worked, fetched good prices in international markets. Today only about three percent of the original kauri forest survives—chiefly in Waipoa and on the Coromandel Peninsula, south and east of Auckland.

To the Maori, the kauri was of great importance, second only to the totara in the variety of its uses. They shaped kauri trunks into war canoes, some of them eighty feet long, and burned kauri gum—congealed sap that fell, cured, and accumulated beneath the trees—at night for lighting.

The first European to make use of kauri wood was probably Marion du Fresne. In 1772 the French commander watched a group of Maori wood-carvers create an elaborate war canoe from a kauri bole. He was impressed by the wood's strength and workability, and ordered his own carpenters to shape a kauri into a foremast. Yellow-brown, straight of grain, light, and resistant to rot, the wood proved well suited to the purpose.

Neither the Maori nor the early French explorers realized it, but the kauri hails from an ancient lineage dating to the dinosaur era. Botanists place the tree in the Araucariaceae, a primitive family that includes the monkey puzzle tree of Chile and the Norfolk Island "pine." *Agathis australis*, the kauri, is found only in New Zealand.

The nearest town was miles away, my stomach was reminding me it was empty, and my throat was dry. Seeking refreshment, I returned to the car, kicked up a cloud of gravel, and rumbled northward.

The Solitaire Guest House, a friendly-looking B&B, soon appeared at a bend in the road. Although it was late afternoon and I was eager to eat and rest, I raced by the place on first look, put off by the elegance of its hand-painted clapboards and encircling porches—manifestations, no doubt, of an expensive nightly rate. I drove a few more miles, found no other options, and returned.

A handsome white-haired woman answered the bell. She hesitated at my request for a single room, then said she could offer me a small bed in a room with a king size. (Seeing my puzzled look, she assured me the king size would remain unoccupied.) The price, $39.50, included a cooked dinner and a hot breakfast. I had blundered upon a bargain.

I must have looked woebegone, because the woman—who introduced herself as Betty White—ushered me immediately down a dark, kauri-paneled hall into a bright common room. Hot tea was being poured into china cups, and a plate of cookies rested on a table.

I was soon shaking the big calloused hand of Betty's husband, Lloyd. Lloyd was cordial, and I liked him at once. He was sitting with three of my fellow guests: Gordon and Bernadette, a lively, well-groomed English couple, retired and living in Whangarei; and Barry, a schoolteacher, a tall, fortyish man with a thick mustache.

"Barry," Lloyd explained to me with a wink, "is a fugitive from justice. He's a schoolteacher who has come here to the valley with two unfortunate colleagues and thirty-eight sixteen-year-olds." That explained the big bus parked outside. "While the others are making a two-day tramp through the bush, poor Barry is 'sleeping on the bus'—or so he has led the others to believe. They will kill him when they find out where he's *really* been staying."

Later, after I had enjoyed a hot shower and a nap, Betty and Lloyd served evening tea—roast beef, potatoes, string beans, and baked pumpkin. Over dessert I raised the subject of kiwi.

Someone told the story of a dog carrying a kiwi home and the owner having it stuffed, but no one at the table had seen a kiwi in the bush. They had heard kiwi squeals at night on numerous occasions, but that was all. "We can offer you sympathy," Lloyd said, "but we can't supply encouragement."

In the morning, after making arrangements to stay a second night, I drove north to take a look at Hokianga Harbor. I pulled off on a sandy shoulder a half hour later. Ahead a placid bay, bright and blue, gave way on the distant shore to a range of sand dunes.

Hokianga is rich in history. On the twelfth of December, 1769, the harbor provided Jean de Surville, a French explorer, with his first glimpse of the New Zealand coastline. Meanwhile, on that same day the English captain James Cook, unaware of de Surville's proximity, was sailing up the Pacific coast of the North Cape. A few days later de Surville's *St. Jean Baptiste* and Cook's *Endeavour* passed near each other in thick fog. Neither ship saw the other.

Sixty-five years later, in 1835, Hokianga was the site of a skirmish between Maori and Europeans known as the "Battle of the Pork." An Anglican parson, angry after the natives had attacked an English sawmill operator and his wife, led a band of forty or fifty of his parishioners into a Maori village. There were no human fatalities on either side, as far as we know, but 150 of the villagers' pigs were killed.

Living near Hokianga in those days was a semimythic figure in early New Zealand history named F. E. Maning. Maning was a tall, burly Irishman who had come to the bay in 1833 from Tasmania. He married the sister of a Maori chief and for years lived among her people. If his own accounts can be believed, Maning plunged into one daring adventure after another. He wrote of his exploits in *Old New Zealand*, a book published in Auckland in 1863.

The volume is a page-turner. Scenes of war and cannibalism are recounted in a nonjudgmental, deadpan style that underscores their horror. For example, there is a story of two settlers who were "hospitably entertained one night by a chief, a very particular friend of mine. . . ." The following morning, the author reports blithely, the chief ate one of them. He did so "to pay himself for his trouble and outlay."

On another occasion Maning attended a ceremony at a Maori village. The formalities were long-winded and made him restless, so when no one was looking he wandered off. Soon he stood on a knoll among a circle of "splendid individuals." They were dressed in "the best sort of ornamental cloaks," and Maning concluded that his companions were "magnates or personages of some kind or other." The tale continues:

As I approached, one of these splendid individuals nodded to me in a very familiar manner, and I, not to appear rude, returned the salute. I stepped into the circle formed by my new friends, and had just commenced a *tena koutou* when a breeze of wind came sighing along the hilltop; my friend nodded again,—his cloak blew to one side. What do I see?—or rather what do I not see? *The head had no body under it!* The heads had all been stuck on slender rods, a cross stick tied on to represent the shoulders, and the cloaks thrown over all in such a natural manner as to deceive anyone.

A weaker man would have fled into the forest. But Maning, curious and fearless (at least in his own account), probed further.

At another place in the village he found an old woman standing beside the severed head of a young man. She wailed sorrowfully, and was slashing herself with an obsidian knife. Maning learned nothing from the old woman, but he made inquiries and found that the head had been severed from the body of one of the woman's sons. In the company of a brother, the young man had been fleeing a group of enemies when a spear struck him in the leg. As he lay bleeding, and the pursuers gained, he cried to his brother, "Do not leave my head as a plaything for the foe." Maning continues, "The brother *did not* deliberate; a few slashes with the tomahawk saved his brother's head, and he escaped with it in his hand, dried it, and brought it home."

Remarkably, these and dozens of similar stories are recounted without editorial comments. Maning, a rarity among the writers of his time, did not look upon the Maori as savages.

Conditions along the shore of Hokianga Harbor haven't changed much since Maning's day. In fact, although the big kauri are gone, the place in other respects is probably wilder than it was then. There are few people here. The lumbermen, the sailors, and the Maori have moved away. The nearest pork is probably a rack of chops in Lloyd and Betty's freezer.

I spent the afternoon lurking in the shade of the Whites'

south porch, writing letters and polishing one of the newspaper columns I was shipping weekly to Connecticut. Lloyd and Betty were busily readying rooms for new guests. I was surprised and pleased when Lloyd appeared in early afternoon bearing a plate of mutton sandwiches.

"I thought you might be needing a bit of lunch," he said. Lloyd was right. I had had nothing to eat, was feeling ravenous, and knew that the nearest restaurant or tearoom was an hour's drive away.

We ate the sandwiches and spent a half hour chatting. Lloyd and Betty had lived near Rotorua, I learned. He was a "truckie" and for years drove freight up and down New Zealand at all hours of the day and night. Several years ago he and Betty inherited the house. Outwardly it was in terrible shape, but a carpenter friend examined it and promised that the basic kauri structure was in fine order. He recommended a facelift, inside and out, and some repairs to the foundation. Thus the Whites found themselves in the renovation business.

After years of hard work the white exterior was crisp and inviting. Inside, the kauri paneling had been brought back to its former elegance by meticulous sanding and rubbing. The house sat at the edge of a broad valley, sunny and fertile, ringed by low hills and bisected by a two-lane road. At the edge of the yard a clear, shallow river, narrow enough to toss a stone across, flowed quietly by. Its banks were lined with American cottonwoods, and in an autumn breeze the leaves of the trees fluttered like pale golden butterflies.

5.

Skull Bay, Tawhiti Rahi.

Below our campsite waves surged against the cliffs. Above us on a steep, bush-covered slope extending to the top of the island, shearwaters in their nesting burrows screamed like ghouls. Silently my seven companions and I gathered around a propane cookstove. Darkness was settling on the bush.

I sat on a plywood box, one of the dozens of pieces of heavy gear we had dragged upslope earlier in the day from our landing site. The others found similar perches.

For the next ten days our research team will eat, sleep, and work on an incline so steep that rolling out of bed would be dangerous. We are camped at a place called Skull Bay, on the island of Tawhiti Rahi, in a small archipelago known as the Poor Knights Islands. Fifteen miles distant, North Island, green and undulating, defines the western horizon.

George spoke softly in Maori. With his eyes closed he faced the summit of the island and addressed his ancestors. He beseeched the "Old People," he later explained, to welcome us to Tawhiti Rahi and to protect us from harm. He told them we had come to study the "lizard" known as the tuatara, and promised that we would leave the islands exactly as we had found them.

A leader of the Ngati-wai, the Maori tribe that once inhabited the Poor Knights, George had joined our expedition as an observer. He wore a faded red T-shirt and denim jeans over a sinewy frame, and he had café-au-lait skin. A set of Fu Manchu whiskers made him appear vaguely oriental.

George joined the expedition chiefly so he could lift a powerful tapu. It had been placed on the Poor Knights by his ancestors about 1808, after the islands' Maori inhabitants had been massacred by an opposing tribe. As far as George knew, no Maori had landed on the island since.

This morning I asked George to tell me the full story. He said that the attackers, who lived near Auckland, had traveled to the Poor Knights and demanded that the islanders give them pigs. But there were no pigs to spare, and the visitors paddled away angry.

Several months later the men of the islands set off in canoes for the mainland. As soon as they were safely out of sight, a Poor Knights slave (belonging to the tribe that had asked for pigs) escaped, stole a canoe, and paddled across the water to his village. There he told his friends and relations that the islands were temporarily undefended.

An attack party was organized. The mainlanders arrived in three canoes during the first black hours of morning. The islanders were asleep, and enjoying the element of surprise, their attackers descended upon them. Women, children, and old men were slaughtered—everyone the mainlanders could find. A few islanders, preferring suicide to slaughter, jumped from the islands' high cliffs onto the rocks below. Others hid in caves. That night the invaders held a *hakari,* or feast. The main course was supplied by (and consisted of) the islanders.

The following morning the mainlanders paddled back to their village. In the bottoms of their canoes they carried leftovers from the previous night's feast, and, alive, the wife of Tatua, the islands' chief.

When the men of the Poor Knights returned, they found

few survivors. Charred bones and dried blood were everywhere. Tatua, grief-stricken and certain that supernatural forces were responsible for the massacre, declared a tapu. This meant that the Poor Knights would never again be inhabited by Maori.

George believed in the tapu. He considered it very powerful, and when he learned that a party of scientists was planning to camp on the islands, he feared for their lives. A tapu rooted in great tragedy, he told me, was not to be taken lightly.

*F*rom first light until dusk, bellbirds skulk ghostlike through the treetops, offering occasional glimpses of their dusky forms. A bellbird is about the size of an American bluebird. It is nothing much to look at—dark, olive backed, with red eyes and a gray-green belly. Thin white streaks like mustaches distinguish the females (the males lack these markings), although they are rarely visible, because bellbirds spend most of their time high in the trees. Like the tuis I saw at Peter Miller's, the bellbirds are honeyeaters. They lap nectar from flowers with their long, brush-tipped tongues.

On North Island bellbirds are rare. But here on the Poor Knights, protected by government regulation (the islands are off limits to all but sanctioned research parties), tapu, and a moat of sea, they flourish.

The Poor Knights bellbirds sing continually, and as vocalists they are inspired. Sir Walter Lawry Buller, the ornithologist, called their sunrise chorale "a morning anthem." James Cook, awakened by bellbirds at an anchorage in Queen Charlotte Sound, compared their singing to "small bells exquisitely tuned."

To my ear these descriptions are apt but understated. My first coherent thought upon waking this morning was that I had died. Surely I was in paradise—liquid, tinkling notes cascaded from the trees above and pooled around me to create a wild, unearthly melody. I closed my eyes and listened, and for an hour drifted, half awake, half asleep in rapture.

6.

Skull Bay, Tawhiti Rahi.

Today two men arrived from the mainland, expanding our research team to ten.

A few notes on the crew:

Alison Cree. Two years ago Alison led the expedition to Stephens Island; she is the person in charge here. Physically she is sturdy, raven haired, and handsome. As a leader she is intelligent and good-humored. I find her excellent company, more relaxed and self-assured than on our last trip together. She is young—twenty-eight—and has a tough job in supervising a team made up mostly of older men, several of them experienced wildlife scientists with their own ideas about doing things. Alison lives with her husband, Marcus, in Wellington. She is a postdoctoral fellow in zoology at Victoria University.

Dave Hunt. A Department of Conservation (DOC) botanist, Dave's regular job is protecting rare plants on Rangitoto Island, near Auckland. This requires that he spend much of his time shooting and otherwise liquidating wallabies, an unsavory chore. The kangaroolike marsupials, introduced from Australia, are destructive to Rangitoto's rare native plants. About thirty-two, Dave is slim, wears a trim sandy beard, and views the world through wire-rimmed glasses. He stands about five feet eight. I found Dave overly serious at first, but upon better acquaintance I have learned that, although hardworking, he is laid-back and good-humored. Dave once taught at a summer camp in Maine.

Richard Parrish. A DOC officer from the Whangarei office, Richard was born in Sussex, England. He retains his Old World accent, keeps hair down to his waist in a ponytail, and has a thick beard streaked with gray. Nearly six feet in height, and of medium build, Richard is probably about forty-two. In manner he can be gruff and aloof, but he sometimes has warmer moments, such as today when he showed me a handful of leaf litter containing "more than a dozen" species of tiny land snails, each no bigger than a pea. Whenever he can, Richard wanders into the bush to go snail hunting.

Mary McIntyre. An entomologist by training, now a research associate in zoology at Victoria University, Mary is reserved, serious, and fortyish. She has curly hair, a pale complexion, and a strong nose. Her gaze is penetrating. Mary spends her free time on the island collecting giant weta—flightless, grasshopperlike creatures that are rare on the mainland.

Steve Thompson. If there is a more pleasant, more unassuming New Zealander than Steve, I haven't met him. He is youthful (about twenty-two), doesn't have a steady job, and like me is here as a volunteer. The most overt humorist in our group, Steve always finds cheerful things to say. I consider him our team's unofficial conciliator and morale officer.

John Newton. Chief of the blood laboratory at Wellington Hospital, John has been helping Alison analyze the blood chemistry of tuatara. Alison invited John to join the trip as a way of saying thanks. John vies with Steve for "most agreeable" honors. Tall, dark (he is part Maori), and exceptionally well mannered, he professes to be in his forties (I disbelieve his claim of having a twenty-one-year-old child) but looks thirty. John calls himself a city person—a rare self-image in New Zealand. He finds the island's numerous mosquitoes (mozzies, he calls them) perplexing, and is not overly fond of the giant poisonous centipedes that occasionally scurry through our campsite. A Buller's shearwater, a large seabird, visits an active nest directly beneath John's tent. Each night it returns to its burrow; the event is a source of great distress for John, and high comedy for the rest of us.

George Parata. I've described George in some detail already. He is good natured, calls everyone mate, and, despite having no formal duties here, goes out of his way to be helpful (catching fresh fish to eat for breakfast, for example). George was not expected to help with our research tasks, but he has proved adept in catching tuatara.

Craig Hodsell. Craig, tanned and boyish, is a DOC officer from Auckland. He could easily pass for a Hyannisport Kennedy—he has the rugged looks, the confidence, the expertise in all things nautical, and an otterlike affinity for water. Reinforcing the image, every article of his clothing is new and of top quality, and each item in his considerable arsenal of camera equipment is the finest Nikon manufactures.

Stanley Palmer. Defying traditional New Zealand reticence, Stanley speaks often and at length. His soliloquies, fortunately, are invariably thoughtful and informative. They take in such subjects as Italian Renaissance painting, the sanitary habits of the Roman upper class, the Boer War, where to find good food in Chicago, the works of Voltaire, island biogeography, and glassblowing. Stanley is neither a boor nor a bore—he thrives on audience participation. He was granted permission to join our landing party in exchange for a promise to supply DOC with the rights to a lithograph—an original work he will create from a Poor Knights scene. (DOC will sell prints to raise funds.) A middle-aged widower with two grown children, Stanley is a well-known artist. He lives in Auckland. In our crew of scientists and nature enthusiasts I find Stanley a refreshing presence—our diet of science grows monotonous at times, and Stanley's talk of art and literature adds welcome seasoning. Like Alison and John, he is a skilled cook. His camp-oven bread, baked daily, is gourmet fare.

Yours truly. How I am perceived I cannot say. I do know that I could have made a better first impression. On the boat that brought us here, the others had their first look at me—puking my guts out over the stern. On Stephens Island, I was part of a small, close-knit team and felt useful and competent. Here, working in an alien environment beside local biologists, I feel as out of place as George Plimpton felt during his short career with the Detroit Lions football team. I am a writer, with no Ph.D., and no vaunted area of expertise. Determinedly stubborn like Plimpton, however, I will persevere.

*I*t is a singular experience to be thrown together on an island for ten days with total strangers (Alison excepted). We eat as a group, commune with nature in the same hand-dug privy (digging it was my contribution to our domestic arrangements), sleep in tents within snoring distance of each other, and work long hours side by side in the bush.

Each day begins in late morning (bedtime typically is three or four A.M.). We rise, one at a time, rummage in the food boxes for our every-man-for-himself breakfasts, and share a "billy" of tea. In the afternoon we swim in Skull Bay or bask like seals on rocks by the shore. Most of our time, however, is spent crashing through the bush. During the day we explore the island, using surveyor's ribbon to mark tracks deep into the interior. (The tracks help us navigate at night.) Despite much hard labor, the company and scenery are congenial, and our days pass quickly.

At night our work is wearying and the clock moves slowly. Thrashing through dense vegetation in pitch darkness, wearing headlamps, we scale heights, detour around cliffs, and scan the island's slopes for tuatara—all while trying to remember the route home to camp. The job is hard, but seeing tuatara and other creatures roaming in primeval forest is abundant compensation for our efforts.

The tuatara of the Poor Knights, I find, are darker than those I saw on Stephens Island. Most of them are graphite colored (the tuatara on Stephens were green), and they are significantly larger. We have caught several that were as long as the distance between John Newton's shoulder and fingertips. John is a big man.

As a child I often burrowed through a neighbor's forsythia bushes on my way home from school. The arching branches formed a perfect tunnel that I loved to crawl through belly-down. Our work here brings back memories of those days. Tawhiti Rahi, the island on which we're camped, is covered with trees, most no more than six or eight feet high. To move among them one must generally walk hunchbacked (at best), or crawl. Already I have accumulated a dozen bleeding scratches of the sort that marked my face and hands often as a boy.

7.

Skull Bay, Tawhiti Rahi.

The Poor Knights are obscure islands. Uninhabited by man for nearly two centuries, lacking natural resources such as precious metals and sandy beaches, and comprising only a few square miles of land, they will never compete for celebrity with Hawaii or the Seychelles. But what Tawhiti Rahi and her sister islands lack in geographical distinction, they more than make up for in the extraordinary plants and animals that occupy their stark volcanic slopes.

The Poor Knights are home to hundreds, perhaps thousands, of tuatara, as well as a nesting colony of some two million Buller's shearwaters. Buller's is a wide ranging but discriminating pelagic bird that chooses to raise its offspring only on the Poor Knights. On the islands, in the bush, there are giant weta and giant centipedes—the former rare, the latter poisonous—and at night we see lizards in such numbers that the ground literally streams with them. The Poor Knights lily, *Xeronema callistemon*, like Buller's shearwater, lives nowhere else. On a daytime hike to the island's high ground Dave, Steve, and I discovered a patch of the lilies. They were great bushy things with long narrow leaves; in form, they resembled clumps of some extravagant grass. Our search for blossoms ended in disappointment—the Poor Knights lily flowers in November, and we were four months late.

Two of the islands cover substantial areas. Tawhiti Rahi,

the largest and northernmost, comprises 318 acres of high plateau (600 feet above sea level) ringed by cliffs. Aorangi, immediately to the south, is about half as large, high on one end and low on the other. Our original plan called for camping on the gentle northern side of Aorangi, but easterly winds on the day we arrived stirred up such a perilous chop at the landing site that venturing ashore was impossible. Alison, thinking quickly and clearly, ordered a change in strategy. We chugged away and disembarked instead at Skull Bay, on the steep but calm western shore of Tawhiti Rahi.

The forest on the islands is dominated by pohutukawa, *Metrosideros excelsa*, a tree that puts forth masses of crimson flowers in December. The pohutukawa are not in bloom, but so densely do they crowd the islands that one can imagine looking down on the islands from a plane at Christmas and interpreting the floral display as a wildfire. The leaves are thick and green, and each appears frosted—as if someone had lightly glazed it with sugar.

Pohutukawa predominates, but other trees thrive scattered among them. We have seen *mapou*, *karaka*, *mahoe*, *kohekohe*, *puriri*, cabbage tree, and four species of tree fern. The handsomest, to my eye, is the puriri.

On a ridge above our camp, several old puriri grow in a sheltered spot. Each can be recognized by its octopus of exposed roots, its stout trunk, and its crown of broad, shiny leaves. The leaves are conspicuously wrinkled, as if they were made of cotton and needed ironing. Purple-pink flowers appear on puriri throughout the year, and as they fall they litter the ground beneath the trees like colored popcorn.

The leafy interior of Tawhiti Rahi is shadowy and mysterious. Along the shoreline the island displays its finest scenery. Skull Bay, the deep cove above which we're camped, is filled with opalescent water that alternates like a chameleon between ultramarine and Nile green. It teems with multicolored fish of many species, and below the water line the walls of the cove bristle with lush submarine vegetation that twists and swirls with the ebbing and surging of the waves. The bay is a fine place for a swim. One can dive with mask and snorkel and see myriad fish, sunbathe on the rocks at the foot of the cliffs, or explore a shoreline pocked with tide pools. The tide pools serve as natural aquaria, and they hold such creatures as pink anemones and scorpion fish.

My favorite way to enjoy Skull Bay is to float on my back in the cool water, gazing up at the cliffs and the sky and the bright austral sun. There are times, alone, late at night, hopelessly mired in dense bush with only a vague idea of my location, when I question my sanity in coming to the Poor Knights. But a minute of backstroking in the cove on a sunny afternoon banishes such thoughts.

This afternoon as I sat on the rocks after a swim, I noticed something gray and smooth amid the aquatic plants at water's edge. It was moving slowly, in perfect synchronization with the waves. Thinking that the object was a plastic rubbish bag gone astray, I climbed down to retrieve it.

To my surprise the thing multiplied several times in size before my eyes, and voluptuous folds of tissue unfurled along the sides. It was a stingray.

The ray's wings rippled gracefully as it swam into open water. It was a marvelously supple creature, and it struck me as a manifestation of pure energy—like a radio wave. With a few more strokes of its wings, the ray vanished into the depths.

Swimming in the bay does wonders for our hygiene. Our work makes us filthy, and each one of us nurses an array of scratches and punctures. I have a nasty gouge on my left cheek, for example, the result of blundering head-on into a broken limb near the rock outcrop we call the Pinnacles. Despite an initial sting, it felt good to cleanse the wound in the sea, and to scrub away the grime surrounding it.

As a result of living on a dry, steep hillside, where every move we make stirs up dust, soil clings to our hair, our clothing, and our skin. Within an hour of arriving we had unwittingly sent every fallen leaf in our campsite on a toboggan ride to the sea. We eat, sleep, and work on exposed soil.

Poor Knights dirt is insubstantial and powdery. It looks, but does not taste, like powdered chocolate, and it floats on the air just as readily. We learn not to look closely at our food and drink, for every piece of buttered bread and each cup of tea is flecked with brown.

Last night, refreshed after a swim and a meal, we divided our group into two parties. One, under the command of Alison, would visit Stack B, a finger of rock rising from the sea near Tawhiti Rahi's western shore. The stack was too steep to land on, so Richard would put the party ashore, then keep vigil in the dinghy. Alison, Steve, and Craig would climb to the summit. (The ascent, up unfamiliar cliffs in the darkness, would require much daring.) Their goal was to see if the stack was inhabited by tuatara. If it was, they would catch the animals they saw, measure them, and bring home samples of their blood.

The second group, of which I was a member, would climb the ridge behind the campsite. Our destination would be a slope pocked with shearwater burrows, near the Pinnacles.

The slope, dusty and dark, was an eerie place to explore in the dead of night. We roamed, each of us alone and out of sight of our colleagues' lights, back and forth through dense bush, twisting, stooping, thrashing, crawling to gain each foot of progress. Several times I climbed over old stone walls. By day I considered such features welcome discoveries, but in the darkness they stirred up images of the 1808 massacre George had vividly described.

After an hour or two on my own, I found myself in a place where the soil was barren of plants, and several enormous boulders—the size of railroad locomotives—stood like monuments. The rocks had been put there by natural forces, I was certain, but in the glow of my headlamp they looked like the famous stone heads of Easter Island. While I searched among them for tuatara, a bird scurried out of the shadows and came to stop beside me.

It was dark, about the size of a quail, with a round body, pointed beak, and red eyes—a spotless crake, a widespread rail of the South Pacific. The bird stood and stared at me, and I stared back. I could almost convince myself that the crake was the spirit of an old Tawhiti Rahi Maori disguised in feathered form.

A pair of tuatara were struggling to escape from the collecting bags that hung on my belt. Seeking John and the others, I left the bird (it turned and ran when I moved) and set off in a direction that I hoped would lead to the track. Suddenly another bird appeared. This one crashed through the branches over my head, came to rest, and looked down at me in surprise. It was much larger than the crake, with a plump, speckled belly and a long, pointed beak—a banded rail. The bird sightings, both so unexpected, gave me the feeling I was being watched.

I bumped into John—literally—near the base of the Pinnacles. Soon afterward, lights brightened the trees around us. Our entire party was reunited a few minutes later.

Dave had bagged four tuatara, John two, and Mary and

George one each. (Stanley, who had accompanied us up the ridge, had returned to camp.) Now the real work would begin.

Our sponsors have not sent us here to admire the flora and fauna and to practice our backstrokes. We are part of an ambitious research program, organized by Charlie Daugherty, Alison Cree, and Mike Thompson, to survey every island inhabited by tuatara. According to the last count, there are twenty-nine where tuatara live. By year's end, scientists will have visited them all.

Launching the program required much effort. Funding was secured from within New Zealand and overseas. Charlie and Alison recruited landing parties for each of the islands, a chore that involved finding dozens of skilled volunteers who would be willing to work hard, under primitive conditions, all night, for no pay. Camping gear—tents, cookstoves, lanterns, tarpaulins, water jugs, cooking utensils, and more—had to be procured in quantities that would allow several parties to venture afield simultaneously. Similar arrangements were made for technical gear. Each landing team needed its own complement of syringes, centrifuges, capillary tubes, measuring tapes, calipers, spring balances, and photographic gear.

On the Poor Knights, Alison kept track of personnel, food, physical amenities, and technical gear with a clear head and a placid temper. Hers was a big job.

At 10:30 p.m., as we sat down to measure and bleed the tuatara we had collected, a metallic object struck the rocks below. The dinghy had returned from Stack B.

We divided our labor. Using spring balances, calipers, rulers, and a measuring tape, John took enough measurements from the tuatara to fit them, if this had been his purpose, with suits. As he finished I took each animal, inserted a syringe, and drew one cc. of blood from its tail. Dave made notes on a clipboard, inked letters and numbers on the flanks of each tuatara, and painted typewriter correction fluid on each animal's snout. Last came Mary. The senior scientist among us, she had won the unsavory job of marking the tuatara permanently by clipping their toes.

What the tuatara thought of our intrusions I cannot say. Most submitted without protest, although several big males squawked noisily and dug sharp claws into our wrists. With these recalcitrant animals I used a trick I had learned on Stephens Island. Hold a tuatara by its torso, swing its tail gently from side to side, and it falls into a trance.

The measuring and bleeding, although briefly unpleasant for the reptiles, is for a good cause. Tuatara are doing well on the Poor Knights, as they are on Stephens Island, but other island populations are in a poor or questionable state. Some of them are nearing extinction—such as on Red Mercury Island, the island I'd be visiting next. In order for the New Zealand Department of Conservation to do an effective job of protecting the tuatara, it must know the reptile's status throughout its sprawling, disjointed range.

Until now a broad, coordinated survey of New Zealand's tuatara islands had never been attempted. Scientists had visited every island at least once but, for the most part, the expeditions had involved different parties using different methods. A few inaccessible islands had not been studied for a decade or two.

This year, within a twelve-month span, scientists would survey every known tuatara population. They would also explore a few islands where tuatara might exist undetected. When all the figures and blood samples were in, the status of the tuatara would at last be clear.

At midnight, our work completed, we dispersed into the bush to return the tuatara to their burrows. This chore occupied more than an hour—crashing at night through trackless bush in search of tiny fluorescent markers wasn't easy. Eventually we hiked down the ridge into camp.

George, who had heard us coming, was boiling water for tea. Pleased by our catch, Alison reported that her team had managed to scale Stack B and collect blood and information from two tuatara. Craig, perched lemurlike in the crotch of a pohutukawa, recounted the details.

George handed me a cup of tea. It was hot and bracing. Stanley brought up Rodin. "Ed, have you seen his bronzes at the Chicago Institute of Art?"

8.

Skull Bay, Tawhiti Rahi, 11 A.M.

Bellbirds chime, the sky is clear and blue, and sunlight trickles through the foliage like green rain. A cool breeze—an early touch of autumn—rustles the walls of my tent. Our food is running low. This morning my ration was a bowl of muesli mixed with reconstituted milk, pear halves (out of a tin), and—Stanley's handiwork—raisin bread. Although it had been cut from a fresh loaf, my buttered bread was liberally seasoned with topsoil.

Two days ago I hiked to the far end of Tawhiti Rahi with Mary. We were the only two in our party who had not, at one time or another, climbed to the island's summit. It was Thursday, and Sunday a boat from the mainland would come to take us away.

We tramped up familiar slopes, past the Pinnacles, to the foot of a high cliff. As we had learned from the others, a gap had opened long ago when the Pinnacles pulled away from the central massif. The gap was heavily vegetated, and up it, holding onto stunted trees and flax, we climbed.

Despite the steepness of the slope, the ascent proved fairly easy. Our chief danger, aside from the possibility of losing a foothold and tumbling downward, was of disturbing wasps in the flax. The day before, not far away, Steve had been stung repeatedly.

Proceeding with care, we reached the high ground safely. The view to the south, when we turned, was dizzying. Far below, dark and flecked with pink, were the tops of the puriri trees. Beyond, the great south ridge, bristling with pohutukawa, dropped toward the sea. The sea was a radiant indigo blue, except along the fringes of the smaller islands, where the waves beat the water to a frothy cream. In the west we could make out the North Island mainland, green and hilly. There were no cities, no visible houses, factories, roads, or airplanes—just bush-clad hills and broad, fertile valleys.

Hiking northward along the plateau proved more difficult than scaling the cliff. We had to detour around several deep chasms and dense patches of bush, and it took us nearly an hour to reach a tiny automated lighthouse at the far end. Along the way the trees, taller than those on the lower slopes, were filled with the chatter of red-crowned parakeets. Occasionally we caught glimpses of the birds' yellow-green feathers, long tails, and vivid scarlet caps as they darted through the branches.

We skirted the edge of a low hillock surrounded by crumbling stone walls. The place was dark and silent, and I detected, as one might recognize the scent of woodsmoke, a palpable melancholy in the air. Wherever we walk on Tawhiti Rahi, I think of the people who fished, farmed, and fornicated here for centuries—and of their gruesome end.

The soil was grayer and drier than what we had encountered below, and it was riddled with seabird burrows—hundreds of thousands of them. We advanced gingerly, taking care not to break through into the birds' nesting chambers. Twice we saw tuatara, but each of the animals ducked into its hole before we could catch it.

We knew we had reached the far end of the island when the foliage brightened, and suddenly we found ourselves at the brink of a cliff. I experienced simultaneous feelings of exhilaration and revulsion, as I always do in such places. Gazing over a brink into the irrevocable, life's choices are never more clearly defined.

From our viewpoint the South Pacific looked like a caricature of an ocean. It was *too* large—so vast that the discovery of New Zealand by Polynesians in canoes struck me as a miracle. It is no surprise that these South Sea islands were settled by man later than any other in Polynesia. Even airline pilots bound for Auckland from afar must grow anxious as they reach New Zealand's latitude and longitude. What if land fails to appear on the radar screen? What then?

After a snack of apples and buttered bread, we turned homeward. Mary, silent on the outward leg of our journey, grew chatty on the return. I learned that I was not the only one "feeling crook" during our voyage to the Poor Knights, and that she cooked in a microwave oven, had a scientist husband, and had been passionately interested in insects since childhood. From time to time during the walk Mary alerted me to examine the big, hard-shelled land snails that littered the ground. The snails, she explained, were *Placostylus hongii*, a vegetarian species of gastropod that fed on fallen leaves. Each of the snails was five or six inches long.

After descending the cleft behind the Pinnacles, we followed a track marked with surveyor's tape back to camp. There the bellbirds greeted us with song.

*L*ast night Alison gave me the night off. I spent most of it in the glow of the lantern, discussing a wide range of subjects with George.

George was enjoying himself immensely, he told me. He was heartened that people had traveled so far, and at considerable expense, to help protect a reptile with no economic value. It gave him hope that the Maori and the Pakeha (European-descended New Zealanders), in seeking to resolve the racial tensions that are developing in his country, would find common ground. He thinks that the beauty and fertility of New Zealand will suffer if the Polynesians and Europeans cannot learn to share the land fairly.

I asked George about racially tainted gang fights, protests, and murders that I had read about in Auckland newspapers. There had been nothing of this sort in the media during my earlier visits—or at least so had been my impression.

"The sesquicentennial of the Treaty of Waitangi will be celebrated next year," George said, "and my people are preparing to make a statement. Unfortunately, people do not always express themselves in a peaceful way. But you will understand. The Maori have spent the last century and a half adjusting to the ways of the Pakeha. Look at the result! The native forests are nearly gone, we are losing our wildlife, and places where the Old People could walk to the sea, throw in a line, and catch a good feed of fish are quickly being stripped bare by nets and the long-line." There was truth to what George was saying. Foreign and domestic fleets, using the latest in technology, were depleting New Zealand's offshore fisheries. Native forests—real bush, not plantations of American pine—were being cut, chopped, and exported by the wood-chipping industry at a shocking rate.

"We've listened to the Pakeha long enough," George said. "Now it's time he listened to us. Seeing all you fellows here, and Alison and Mary, is making me optimistic that the things which must change actually will."

Like George, I too feel certain that the Maori will settle their differences with the Europeans. Although New Zealand has its troubles, it lags far behind other nations in screwing itself up—in overpopulating, in overindustrializing, in despoiling countryside with trash and poison. The country still possesses an abundance of land with a modest number of people living on it. If the New Zealanders cannot learn to coexist peacefully with each other and their environment, no people can.

Yesterday Craig, looking like young Jack Kennedy at the helm of *PT-109*, ferried John, Stanley, and me to Aorangi in the dinghy.

We landed by jumping out of the boat onto a wall of blistered rock. For several hundred yards inland from the shore the bedrock, a type of scoria, was ruddy and riddled with holes. Some of the holes were as tiny as finger marks in sand; others were the size of Olympic swimming pools. The larger basins were filled with water of such clarity that one would have hesitated to dive in for fear that they were dry. In several, big multicolored fish swam in circles. The walls of the pools bristled with bright pink anemones.

Into the biggest basin we plunged. The water was warm—almost hot—and I felt, as I brushed past one gaudy fish after another, that I was swimming in a huge aquarium. I wondered what George's ancestors thought of these pools. After a day digging kumara on the high terraces, natural hot tubs such as these would have been hard to resist.

There was nothing for us to do on Aorangi but relax and explore. Earlier in the week Alison had led a party to the island, and during the course of two long nights they collected dozens of measurements and blood samples. On this day our instructions had been explicit: "enjoy yourselves."

The beach—nothing more than a hard, abrasive lava flow that sloped toward the water—rose gently from the sea to the edge of a forest. Trees filled the island's central basin, and beyond, a ridge of pale rock swept in a great arc from east to west. Above our landing site the west end of the ridge formed a high promontory.

Walking without shoes, I picked my way carefully over the sharp rock to a shallow freshwater pond. It was fed by a stream trickling out of the bush, and its surface was clotted with lime green algae. Growing from crevices beside the pool were familiar wildflowers. I was surprised to find yarrow and ox-eye daisy—European weeds that grow between cracks in Manhattan's sidewalks.

The alien plants of Aorangi brought to mind one other that I had seen on these islands—marijuana. In a bush-choked gully near our latrine, Dave found a plantation, as he called it, of about a dozen cannabis plants. They were about six feet tall, a credit to an absent gardener who had left behind a half-filled sack of fertilizer. I couldn't help but chuckle upon learn-

ing of the find, but Alison was quick to remind me that marijuana farming on the island was no laughing matter. Even if
direct disturbance to the rare plants and animals by the cannabis
growers was minimal, any unauthorized landing could lead to
an accidental wildfire, or result in the introduction to the islands
of rats or cats. The marijuana plants were uprooted, and a
report was sent via radio to authorities on the mainland.

We leave the island tomorrow. I am loath to go. Some
aspects of our life have taken getting used to—the slope of
our campsite, the dirt in our food, the physical and mental
demands of night work in difficult terrain. But now, adjust-
ments made, I feel at peace, blissfully in tune with the dawn
bellbird chorus and with the steady hushed clamor of the surf.

9.

Auckland.

At Whitcoulls, a big downtown bookstore, I purchased a copy
of the homesick American's companion—the *International
Herald Tribune*. The price was $2.75 (highway robbery), the
news stale. From the United States the chief report concerned
former Senator John Tower, who had been chosen by President
Bush to oversee the Department of Defense. Critics were accusing the nominee of actions not befitting the custodian of a
nuclear arsenal, among them excessive drinking and wom-
anizing. Reading the news, I am glad that home is ten thousand
miles away.

In a bottle shop on Queen Street I bought a six-pack of Steinlager. I carried the beer through the lunch-hour crowd on the sidewalks and walked about a mile to Stanley Palmer's house in Mt. Eden.

When I arrived, John Newton was sitting in the kitchen with his own supply of beer. Stanley had remained in the north, visiting friends in Whangarei, but he insisted that John and I enjoy the comforts of his home during our stay in Auckland. (John was resting for a night on his way home to Wellington. I was in transit to another island.) Use of the place came with a single caveat: we must be sure to introduce ourselves to Stanley's roommate, a young woman named Annie.

When I rang the bell at 10:30 P.M., Annie welcomed me graciously. "Yes," she said, "Stanley telephoned earlier and said that people might be coming. Of course you should come right in."

Annie would have been justified in turning me away. Covered with ten days' accumulated grime and beard, I was dressed in clothes that were as fragrant as they were dirty. On one cheek I had a jagged gash, and my hands were covered with scratches. Diplomatically, Annie presented me with a towel and pointed the way to the bath.

In the tub, I rediscovered two of civilization's greatest blessings—soap and hot water. I soaked myself for thirty minutes and emerged feeling spiritually, as well as epidermically, radiant. Luckily, in the bottom of my pack I had a complete set of clean clothes.

When I emerged, Annie offered me a cup of tea. We drained a pot, sitting at a big wooden table in the kitchen, while I learned something of Annie's life. She was in her thirties and, like Stanley, was a printmaker. She was also a "bush carpenter," and had recently hammered together a "bach," or bungalow, for herself on Great Barrier Island. Then it was my turn. Annie, my first postexpedition audience, listened gamely to tales of tuatara, topsoil, and bellbirds.

Before going to bed, Annie gave me a tour of the house, an old two-story structure on a quiet Auckland side street. Upstairs, in addition to the kitchen and the bathtub I had seen already, were a cozy library equipped with a color television, two bedrooms (Annie's, and Stanley's across the hall), and a large room beside the bath that was filled with racks of Stanley's lithographs. Downstairs Annie showed me a washing machine and provided instruction in its idiosyncrasies.

The cellar of the house had a concrete floor. It was occupied by a variety of big cast-iron machines that Stanley used to create lithographs.

Annie was surprised by my ignorance of Stanley's reputation. She explained that he was an artist of considerable repute, and showed me a dozen of his lithographs where they hung in an upstairs hallway. I needed no further convincing, but Annie produced a coffee-table book featuring the work of prominent New Zealand printmakers. In it I found the work, and the familiar face, of a man I knew best as a baker of raisin bread.

*T*onight John caught a plane to Wellington, Annie dined with friends, and I took a stroll alone through Mt. Eden. A touch of rouge lingered in the western sky, and Auckland's myriad lights glittered in the distance as if the valley had been overrun with glowworms.

Until I reached a busy thoroughfare, the only fellow creature I encountered on my walk was a brush-tailed possum. It had been squashed by a car. The houses along the street were mostly low wooden structures, and each possessed the same idiosyncratic, homemade quality that I admire in old dwellings in the American South.

For my tea I purchased an enormous greasy carton of prawn chow mein. The take-away counter where I bought it was spattered with cooking oil, and the oil had captured road dust the way a spider web collects flies. The name of the place struck me as cryptic—"King of Kings."

Tomorrow I leave for Red Mercury Island.

10.

Red Mercury Island.

Fifty miles south and east of Auckland, the Coromandel Peninsula splits from the mainland and juts northward into the South Pacific. A map of the area that includes New Zealand's biggest city and the peninsula resembles the upturned palm of a right hand. Auckland occupies the thick inner joints of middle and forefingers. Piha, where Peter Miller lives, rests on the tip of your pinkie. The thumb, from base to nail, is the Coromandel Peninsula. Somewhere between the thumb's knuckles, on the outer side, is the quiet seaside resort of Whitianga.

This morning, as the day dawned gray and cool, I arrived in Whitianga with Mary McIntyre (who had worked with us on the Poor Knights) and Ian MacFadden. Ian, a DOC field biologist, had driven us from Auckland.

A dozen men and women—the rest of our team—stood

on the village pier. We introduced ourselves, shook hands, and carried our gear down a steep flight of steps into the hold of the boat. White and blue and fitted with a canopy to match, it was a tourist vessel chartered for the occasion. In a few minutes we were under way.

Our destination was a chain of volcanic islands, nineteen miles to the north and west. To reach them we first had to churn across Mercury Bay.

The word *mercury* is part of many place-names in this part of New Zealand. Near Whitianga, during his first expedition to the South Pacific, James Cook observed the transit of the planet Mercury. It was an important achievement—the sighting allowed Cook to compute his latitude—and he celebrated it by adding "mercury" to the names of numerous local features.

According to plan, upon reaching the Mercuries we would divide into several independent parties, each to disembark on a different island. I was bound for Red Mercury Island, the outermost of the chain. There for a week I would hunt, catch, and examine tuatara. (Unofficially, I also aimed to search for kiwi.)

I was one-quarter of a foursome otherwise made up of New Zealand wildlife scientists. Until a recent government reorganization, my three companions—Jim Jolly, Rogan Colbourne, and Graeme Taylor—had been employed by the New Zealand Wildlife Service. Recently that bureaucracy had been absorbed by the newly created New Zealand Department of Conservation, and Jim and Graeme lost their jobs. Rogan was the only man among us on the payroll. Like me, Jim and Graeme were here as volunteers.

Jim was a wiry, fortyish man with a neat beard and a voice so soft it was often inaudible. Rogan was tall, dark, and angular, and he was also soft-spoken. Graeme had thinning blond hair, a thick red-brown beard, and, unlike his colleagues, possessed a booming voice. To the same degree that Jim and Rogan were reticent, Graeme was expressive. I had heard his views, by the time we lowered the dinghy off Red Mercury Island, on matters ranging from New Zealand's economic prospects ("bloody horrible") to the nesting behavior ("bloody interesting") of the Pycroft's petrel.

The air was raw. I had goose bumps. A chill autumn wind, blowing straight out of Antarctica, was quickly sapping my optimism. Tawhiti Rahi had presented its grandest profile upon our arrival, rising from the sea like some grand Polynesian ziggurat, but Red Mercury appeared low and worn. The landing beach was covered with polished black boulders that looked like dead porpoises.

A light drizzle fell during the two hours it took us to haul our gear to a campsite a hundred yards inland. We pitched tents in a flat, grassy place where Jim and Rogan had camped before and hung a tarpaulin under which to cook, eat, and stow equipment. A stream flowed nearby; Jim said it would be our source of drinking water.

In the pohutukawa trees around the campsite a half dozen birds, hidden by leaves, produced sounds that were grating and mechanical. They had starting making noise as we stepped ashore, and now their calls were growing louder. I asked the others if they could tell me what kind of bird was making the ruckus.

"Those are New Zealand saddlebacks," Jim said matter-of-factly. I was astonished—by Jim's manner, as well as by the identity of the birds. Saddlebacks are extremely rare. They are black, crowlike birds with fleshy wattles near their mouths, and patches of rust-colored feathers on their backs that resemble saddles. No saddlebacks survive on the mainland, but they still exist on a few offshore islands—including Red Mercury.

"The song of the saddleback," Jim continued, "sounds like the starter motor of an old truck. Listen." He was right. Scanning the forest with my ears, I was pleased to hear starter motors everywhere.

Our team included a fifth member that I have neglected to mention: Tess, a golden Labrador retriever. She was, Rogan said upon my asking, "a kiwi dog," a bona fide specialist in tracking the national symbol. Perhaps, I hoped, Tess could teach me a few tricks.

Kiwi have lived on Red Mercury Island since July 1983. At that time scientists aiming to establish a new population released twelve of the rare little spotted kiwi (six of each sex) on the island. My colleagues refer to the birds as little spots.

At the time of the introduction, the world's only self-sustaining population of little spotted kiwi lived on Kapiti Island, a 4,900-acre refuge off North Island's southwest coast. There the birds flourished, but it was decided to remove some of them to other islands as an insurance against catastrophe. Like tuatara, flightless birds on islands are vulnerable to fire and the introduction (accidental or otherwise) of exotic mammals. By establishing little spotted kiwi populations on several islands, New Zealand wildlife authorities hoped to safeguard the future of the species. If disaster struck one of the islands, other populations of little spotted kiwi would survive.

Although our chief role here is to find, measure, and take blood samples from tuatara, we will also attempt to count the island's kiwi. There should be little conflict between the tasks. Kiwi, like tuatara, are active at night, so it will be possible to look and listen for the bird while we search burrow-pocked slopes for the reptile. And there may not be enough tuatara on the 509-acre island to keep us occupied—only four have ever been found here. Tuatara are scarce, apparently, because the island teems with rats.

While blame for most of New Zealand's ecological woes can be placed on the Europeans, the Maori are not blameless. They imported the *kiore*, the Polynesian rat, and apparently they did it intentionally. The rat was remarkably fecund, able to survive just about anywhere and, most important to the Polynesians, edible. Kiore were tender and pleasantly flavored. The Maori snared them in traps, roasted them over fires, and ate them muscle, viscera, and all.

Having been given a beachhead, the kiore spread to every place the Maori lived and hunted—over North and South islands, and to smaller coastal islands as well. Zoologists suspect that the kiore—perhaps aided by other introduced mammals— eliminated the tuatara, the Stephens Island frog, and several native lizards from the New Zealand mainland.

But even villains have enemies. When James Cook unwittingly unloaded a cargo of ship rats in Pickersgill Harbor, easy living for kiore in New Zealand came to an abrupt end. The new arrivals were more aggressive and efficient than their Polynesian cousins, and they immediately set about killing and devouring every kiore they could find. Ship rats were soon joined by another European species, the Norway rat. Both of the newcomers wreaked havoc on native birds, reptiles, amphibians, and invertebrates.

Today on North and South islands ship and Norway rats thrive. Kiore survive only on offshore islands. Seven of the islands inhabited by tuatara are also populated by kiore.

The rats and the reptiles do not get along. On tuatara

islands where kiore are established, young tuatara are absent and the number of adults steadily declines. Kiore are chiefly vegetarian, but somehow they prevent tuatara from reproducing, perhaps by eating their eggs and young. (The exact nature of their impact is unknown.) As old tuatara die of natural causes, their population on a kiore-inhabited island will slowly diminish by attrition.

This is happening in the Mercuries. Three islands are home to tuatara, and two of these—Middle and Green islands, which are free of rats—sustain the reptiles in abundance. On the third, Red Mercury, the scurrying and squeaking of rats is often heard in the bush after dark.

We found a tuatara tonight on the brink of a cliff north of camp. In the darkness we had been searching a "clear" (a crescent of exposed red rock and soil) high above Von Luckner's Cove, the island's deepest bay. Jim had been sweeping one end of the open area with his headlamp while I was scrutinizing the other.

Suddenly he shouted, "I've got one. What shall I do—catch it?" Jim's words gave me pause. Although it had not been clear to me until now, I, by virtue of my experience on Stephens Island and the Poor Knights, would have to lead the others in tuatara work. The sole outsider in a group of veteran New Zealand scientists, I was stuck in an awkward position.

"Yes," I answered. "Get hold of it if you can. We'll put it in a collecting bag and take it back to camp."

Jim's tuatara was a thin, wrinkled male, so dark that it was nearly black. In temperament it was listless—the animal exhibited none of the kicking, clawing, and squawking of its Poor Knights cousins. After finding that the tuatara weighed only 650 grams (just under a pound and a half), I felt guilty robbing it of blood.

Our chief excitement tonight was generated not by tuatara but by a kiwi. On our return journey from the clear, Jim and I stopped at a place in the jungle where a tattered piece of surveyor's tape dangled from a branch. The spot, Jim said, was a listening post.

We listened. For nearly an hour we heard nothing that could be construed as a kiwi. There was plenty of noise, however. All around us things squeaked and rustled in the leaves. I asked Jim what they were. "Rats," he said. We also heard a single abrupt cry that Jim said was given by a morepork (the native owl). For an hour the only other sounds emanated from raindrops tapping on the leaves, from the surf, and from our own breathing.

Suddenly from the east came a faint cry, shrill and rising. "A kiwi," Jim whispered. "A male."

That was all. The bird never squealed again, nor did it materialize in the glow of our headlamps. I could hardly believe that I had heard it.

11.

Red Mercury Island.

Today, beneath our dining fly, Rogan found a sharp, curving fragment of obsidian. The rock, black and glasslike, does not occur here naturally. A former islander imported it, likely from Mayor Island to the south. Obsidian was prized for making tools.

The Maori knew Red Mercury as Whakau. The island was uninhabited when the Europeans arrived, but archeologists exploring the bush here have found an array of stone walls, earthen terraces, and rubbish middens.

Restless, and eager to explore my surroundings by daylight, I hiked this morning into the jungle. My plan, if I could find my way, was to walk up and over the hump of the island to a bay on the northern shore.

The place had caught my eye on Rogan's map, on which it was labeled Von Luckner's Cove. Count Felix Von Luckner, whose nickname was the "Sea Devil," was a German naval captain in World War I. He had been captured by the British in Fiji and taken to New Zealand. One night he and several men escaped from an Auckland prison, stole a boat, and sailed into the South Pacific. While an unsuccessful search for him was mounted, Von Luckner hid out on Red Mercury Island, in the cove that bears his name. Several days later he put to sea again. He was captured by the New Zealand authorities shortly afterward.

Getting to the cove wasn't easy. On the map, it seemed to require only hiking a short way east along the south beach to the mouth of a stream, following the watercourse to its upper reaches, and striking off through the jungle to the north and east. Hitting the cove, which is surrounded by cliffs, promised to be a sure thing.

Because of the fairly dry weather of recent weeks, the stream had become a mossy ditch punctuated by occasional puddles. The mossy ditch branched again and again, and soon, deciding which tine of a fork was the main channel (the one drawn on the map) was impossible. To make matters worse, the stream course ran through thickets, forcing me to choose repeatedly between trying to crash through a tangle on a sure course, or to attempt circumventing it, in hopes of relocating the ditch upstream.

When I could follow the stream no more, I took aim for the north and east. At first, walking overland, the going was easy. The trees were mostly tall spindly pohutukawa with little understory beneath, and the slope was gentle. But on high ground I found myself hopelessly mired in a thicket.

Sunlight poured through a hole in the canopy. If I was a bird, I would have flown and been free in a second. As it was, I pushed forward through the undergrowth. Unfortunately, the farther I pushed, the more dense the vegetation became. Eventually I could advance no more, stuck in a patch of flax eight feet high.

One useful thing I had learned on the Poor Knights was to be careful in flax. Armed with this intelligence, I was ready when a squadron of wasps swarmed toward me. I ran—or tried to.

Flailing my arms and legs, with my body nearly horizontal like a swimmer's, I managed to outdistance the wasps without getting stung. Soon I found myself in another thicket more dense than the first.

Ten minutes of crawling brought me to a place where I could get off my belly and stand. I considered returning to camp but decided against it. There was no guarantee that retreat would free me from the bush any sooner than continuing onward. I crashed ahead through brush, circling the flax to the east. In little time I found myself standing on a cliff overlooking the cove.

The flanking walls of Von Luckner's cove, walls of vertical rock, rose several hundred feet out of the sea. By chance I had broken out of vegetation at the head of the embayment, where the wall was less steep. I picked my way slowly downward, holding onto trees that were rooted in the crumbling rock and using crevices as footholds. Soon I was safe at the bottom.

The cove, I could see, was an ideal hideout. The inner reaches were hidden from the sea by headlands, and the water, open to the north, was well defended against southerly gales. I sat and ate a sandwich on a boulder warmed by sunshine. For a moment I thought I heard organ music—deep, thundering chords that reverberated from the cliffs.

Tonight Jim invited me to accompany him on a kiwi-listening foray to a headland west of camp. Afterward, he said, we could hike to a hillside marked on the map as "Roly Poly." The slopes there were riddled with bird burrows. It sounded like perfect habitat for tuatara.

An hour after tea, Jim and I were standing waist deep in grass on the island's southwest corner. The sun, yellow and soft like warm butter, was melting onto the mainland in the west. Above, the sky was clear, and one by one we watched the stars of the Southern Cross twinkle into view.

As we waited for darkness, Jim told me about his past. He had grown up in the Midlands of England, become an avid rock climber, and graduated from a university with a bachelor's degree in biology. There were no jobs, and he hadn't been sure what to do. His father suggested a plan: he would pay Jim's fare to New Zealand, and Jim could work, do some mountain climbing, and earn his ticket home.

Jim accepted the offer but never went back. He loved New Zealand, the open spaces and the wildlife. "Quite sad, really," Jim said. "The old man died two years after I left. I never saw him again."

A dozen yards to my right, Jim blew on a shepherd's

whistle. He was imitating little spotted kiwi, hoping to provoke a response.

Jim said that if a kiwi appeared nearby, I should try to catch it. With the bird in hand, he could assess its general health and see if it wore a leg band. A band would indicate that the kiwi was one of the original transplants from Kapiti Island. The lack of a band would mean good news—that a pair of the Kapiti birds had produced offspring.

Jim told me how to catch a kiwi if I had an opportunity to try. "Remain still. They don't see well and will sometimes run into you. If a bird comes close, get your arms around it and pin it to the ground as quickly as you can. Then be sure to hold its legs."

I had read somewhere that kiwi had sharp spurs on their legs—spurs capable of inflicting serious wounds. I asked Jim about this.

"Rubbish. I've never been hurt. Just grab the kiwi firmly, and hold his legs. If you don't, you'll find yourself with nothing but feathers."

Suddenly a sharp trill rang out. It came from nearby, from somewhere in the bush beyond the clearing. My heart pounded.

Jim whistled again. The kiwi replied, then began to call repeatedly. With each blast its voice grew louder and closer. At any moment I expected the animal to part the grass before me.

But it never did. The calling died out. "I've taken a bearing on the bird's direction," Jim said, compass still in hand. "Rogan, who likely heard it, too, will have done the same. We'll use those bearings to draw lines on the map, beginning from locations we can pinpoint—the listening posts. Rogan is further along the ridge. The place where his line intersects mine will tell us the location of the kiwi at the time it was calling."

I wouldn't have thought it possible to track birds as secretive as kiwi without fitting them with radio transmitters.
But Jim and Rogan, during their earlier work on Kapiti Island,
had found a way to get the job done using simple triangulation.
The method was ingenious. By week's end they would be able
to estimate the number of kiwi on the island, and to draw a
rough map of their territories.

By the time Jim had recorded the compass setting, darkness had fallen on the bush. We set off to the north, picking
our way through a thicket while keeping safely back from the
cliffs. Eventually we descended a steep bank under tall trees
and set off across a flat terrace.

The terrace took ten minutes to traverse. During the walk
I thought of the islanders who had once grown sweet potatoes
in the soil under our feet. If Von Luckner could hide here
successfully, so could the Maori. What would I do if a tattooed
face appeared in my headlamp? Ahead there was only darkness
and more darkness, the stuff of speculation.

Kiore were everywhere. For every rat we saw we heard
dozens, rattling through the dry fallen leaves. Their eyes
glowed like embers in our lights.

At the place known as Roly Poly, Jim and I separated. A
convex slope of bare, powdery soil and old gnarled trees curved
up and out of sight. It was riddled with burrows—thousands
of them. This was the kind of place tuatara would inhabit in
great numbers on an island free of rats.

I ascended the left side of the bank. Jim worked his way
up the right. I trained my beam on every burrow I saw and
peered into crevices among the exposed roots of trees. The soil,
as light and powdery as moon dust, muffled my footsteps. The
only sounds were the distant cries of seabirds. Occasionally a
rat blundered into view, raced across the pool of light thrown
by my headlamp, and fled into the darkness.

I had been optimistic about finding tuatara at Roly Poly, regardless of the dearth of reptiles on the island reported by earlier researchers. The Swiss-cheese slope was a tuatara paradise, as full of holes and nooks between roots as the high ground of Tawhiti Rahi. But we found nothing. There was not even a tatter of shed skin, or a line of footprints in the soil.

The Maori, who imported the kiore, had had no intention of harming the tuatara. In their culture the tuatara was sacred and forbidden. Only the earliest of the Polynesian inhabitants of New Zealand dared eat them, and afterward, in later centuries, the practice died out.

I find myself speculating about the tuatara's future. Will man be able to halt the reptile's decline on islands shared by rats? It isn't likely, at least on the larger islands. Rats can usually reproduce faster than they can be killed off, and trapping or poisoning the rats of an entire island is costly, in manpower as well as dollars. Can mammals be prevented indefinitely from reaching islands such as the Poor Knights that now provide tuatara safe haven? No one knows. The tuatara islands are spread out over a vast area. It would require an entire navy to patrol them effectively.

12.

Red Mercury Island.

"I can't promise you'll see a kiwi, but if you don't mind doing a bit of bush bashing, yes, you're welcome to come along."

Rogan's tanned face cracked a rare smile. He was a reserved, intensely private man about the age of thirty. With Tess, the kiwi dog, he was soon to depart for the high ground north and west of camp.

Just past noon we were off. Tess led the way, looking uncomfortable in a steel muzzle. Rogan explained that Tess had never hurt a kiwi (in his opinion she never would), but a little spotted kiwi had been killed recently by another tracking dog. The muzzle was a necessary precaution.

Over mossy ground, under a tangle of vines and foliage, through a tangle of pohutukawa and tree fern, we followed a stream up the island's central valley. At times we were forced to jump to the opposite bank, and to cross again, in order to bypass impenetrable thickets of bracken.

"Tess, good girl. Find us a kiwi."

Waving her tail, Tess dog raced off, ears flapping, nose to the ground. Back and forth she swept, sniffing, listening, poking her muzzle into burrows. We did our best to track the dog by sight, sound, and guesswork.

The going was rough. Keeping up with Tess meant abandoning our old route—the path of least resistance—and picking our way through masses of fallen trees.

High on the ridge we briefly lost the sight and sound of Tess. Eventually we found her at the base of an old tree. Her head and forequarters were buried in a dark opening framed by roots, and her tail wagged excitedly.

"Good girl, Tess." Rogan nudged the dog aside and stuffed his own head and shoulders into the void. (Lucky for him, I thought, New Zealand has no bears, no badgers, no rattlesnakes.)

Tess and I waited as Rogan's legs and torso twisted at our feet. With a flashlight he was searching the hollow for signs of kiwi. A few feathers, or feces, would tell him the burrow had once been occupied. But Rogan was hopeful he would discover a sleeping bird. Kiwi are nocturnal. They hole up in dens during the daytime.

Rogan emerged dirty and crestfallen. "No one's at home. But I found bits of feather, several droppings, and a fragment of eggshell. A kiwi's been here, all right."

The feathers he placed in my hand looked at a glance like wisps of fine gray hair. I looked more closely. The "hairs" branched into barbs, as real hair would never do. I asked about the shell, which was greenish white. "Is this an old shell, Rogan, or is it fresh?"

"Old, I suspect by the look of it."

We resumed our search, Tess leading the way. As we walked, Rogan explained that kiwi nest throughout the year. They have no single breeding season, although most eggs are produced in winter, spring, and summer (July through February).

Female kiwi are larger than male kiwi, Rogan said. A little spotted hen is about the size of a domestic chicken. She lays an egg that weighs a quarter to a third of her own body weight—the biggest egg, proportionately, in the bird world. Kiwi produce one egg at a time.

After the egg is laid, the male kiwi does all or most of the incubating. Meanwhile the female, exhausted and depleted, plunges into the bush, feeds actively, and replenishes her reserves of fat and calcium.

The male kiwi has a long wait. The embryo inside the egg takes more than two months, and sometimes nearly three, to develop. During that time the male must sit on the egg by day, and at night leave it untended so he can hunt for food to sustain himself. The male may lose half his body weight before the job is done.

At hatching time the kiwi chick, lacking the egg tooth

of other birds, kicks its way out of the shell with its powerful legs and feet. Rogan said that the young kiwi leaves the burrow and begins feeding beside its parents a week or two after hatching.

"Who feeds the hatchling during the first days?"

Rogan paused. "We don't really know. You see, kiwi, as nocturnal birds, are bloody difficult to observe. And their environment"—he gestured at the mass of limbs and leaves that surrounded us—"doesn't make our work easy. We still have a great deal to learn. We do know that a newly hatched kiwi carries a yolk sack, like a hatchling reptile. This may serve as a temporary food supply. It's conceivable, actually, that parent kiwi don't feed their young at all."

Back at camp the main course of our evening tea was a lump of beef that hadn't been refrigerated for a week. Jim cooked it with vegetables in a covered pot. By the time he pronounced the meal ready, the pot's contents had taken on the gray-brown color of the soil underfoot, and the smell was appallingly cadaverous.

It was easy to understand how the Maori living on these islands turned to devouring each other. The bush offers few temptations—there are no conspicuous animals, no tropical fruits, no succulent stalks ready for the picking. There was fern root, which the Maori ate for starch, but that must have grown tiresome. *Ah, for something fresh!*

After scrubbing the dishes and stuffing our packs with gear, Graeme and I set out for Von Luckner's Cove. Our plan was to traverse the island before dark, search the clears above the cove for tuatara as soon as the sun went down, and spend the rest of the night hunting for tuatara in the interior bush.

The waning sun followed us into the jungle, painting our backs and the leaves of the pohutukawa in amber. As the bush thickened behind us, the sun could no longer keep up. It transformed itself into a soft greenish light, which radiated from all directions as if the trees themselves were luminous. Saddlebacks squawked and bellbirds chimed.

Straying eastward away from the streambed, missing a fork to the left, we were soon mired in vines and branches (rubbish, Graeme called it). At last we broke into open forest, hiked a few minutes farther upslope, and emerged on a cliff top overlooking the cove.

There we sat on warm rocks, awaiting the darkness. The moon was rising in the east, while to the north and west the salmon-colored sky was fading into deep indigo. The moon brightened rapidly, slowing the transition from day to night.

We heard a man-made sound. A boat chugged around the eastern headland and into the cove. There were no running lights, and the cabin was dark—odd, unless we were looking at a ghost ship.

"Von Luckner?" Graeme said, wondering out loud. "Or smugglers? Oh, I suppose it's just a fisherman taking shelter for the night. But it's bloody odd that he's switched his lights off."

A rasping noise joined the slow thumping of the engine. An anchor was being lowered. The motor coughed and was silent.

I flashed a light at the boat. No response came. Graeme laughed. "If it is Von Luckner, perhaps we'd better leave him in peace."

We searched the clear, found nothing, then entered the bush. The darkness among the trees was profound. Walking along with my headlamp pointing the way, I felt like a diver immersed in black ink.

We split up. I dipped down the hill to avoid rubbish and

soon lost all sense of direction. Graeme's light had vanished, and for a moment I nearly panicked. The visible world consisted of nothing more than a claustrophobic circle defined by my light. Beyond, a wall of blackness loomed.

I wanted to cry out but hesitated. Less than a mile from camp, I was in no real danger. The weather was mild, there was a raincoat in my pack, and the most dangerous animal on the island was a rat the size of a chipmunk. At worst, I reassured myself, if I remained hopelessly disoriented I could spend the night in a tree, sleep if I could, and trudge back to camp after daybreak.

Although the facts were reassuring, I still felt anxious. Perhaps this was because once, when I was a boy of five, a gang of older boys with whom I was hiking ran off through the forest and left me alone and frightened, unable to catch up. Darkness was coming fast and home was far away along unfamiliar paths.

On that occasion, as on this, I was in no immediate danger. But I was frightened—there were poisonous snakes in those American woods, as well as foxes, bobcats, and feral dogs. I was a little boy in a culture where children were taught to be afraid of the woods at night.

In the years since, I had passed dozens of nights in forests. I fished for bass, hiked under full moons, photographed owls, searched for flying squirrels and bats, drank beer, and courted girlfriends. Always I had been accompanied by someone—a man, a woman, a dog. But solitary travel in the woods at night was alien to me. I was getting edgy.

Graeme eventually appeared. By that time I had found my way back to higher ground and rediscovered my nerve.

Later that night Graeme and I became entangled in more rubbish. For nearly an hour we crashed left and right, failing again and again to break free. We crawled on our bellies, plowed face-first through sharp underbrush, and eventually lost our sense of direction.

Suddenly Graeme, his headlamp visible ahead of me, howled. "I've lost my bloody glasses. I'm blind as a bat without them."

Our predicament was so absurdly hopeless that we laughed. If the glasses couldn't be found I, who even in daylight had trouble making sense of the island's terrain, would by default assume the job of finding our route back to camp. Graeme saw so poorly without glasses that he said I would have to lead him by the hand.

We searched and searched, Graeme able to focus on objects only within a few inches of his nose. He moaned in frustration. The glasses would cost several hundred dollars to replace. If we failed to find them now, relocating this place in the morning to resume the search might be impossible.

Just then I caught a glint of polished brass in a clump of bracken—the glasses. Graeme was warmly appreciative. "Good one!" he said.

Eventually we escaped the bush and climbed back to the clearing above the cove. It was good to stand in the open again, to look out over the water and breathe the salty air. The cliffs on the west side of the cove appeared gothic and forbidding in the moonlight. Below, rocking on the calm water, the mysterious boat creaked against its anchor rope.

We searched the clear and two others like it. There were no tuatara. At the north end of the third, we crashed back into the bush and resumed hunting. No tuatara. After an hour we stopped to rest, collapsing on a smooth bank of soil riddled with burrows. Soon we would start back to camp.

Without warning, Graeme leapt to his feet and bolted into the darkness. He was shouting something, but I couldn't make out the words.

I charged into the bush, hurrying to catch him. A glimmer of light on the trunks of distant trees provided my only clue to Graeme's whereabouts. In a few minutes I found him leaning against a tree, gasping for wind.

"I tried to grab the bastard but he got away."

"Who got away?"

"A kiwi." Graeme was so winded he could hardly get out the words.

"Where is it?"

"That way." As quickly as Graeme could raise his arm to point, I was off and running.

Twice I had traveled to New Zealand with high hopes of seeing the national bird. Twice I had failed. This was my third chance, and I was determined to make the best of it. Determination made me fearless. The prospects of getting lost or mired in rubbish no longer seemed bugbears.

Into the night I sprinted—up the slope, over logs, under branches, around vines. I could hear something kicking up the leaves ahead. It was making a snuffling sound.

Suddenly, on the far side of a fallen tree, a creature straight from the imagination of Dr. Seuss materialized.

I had seen kiwi in zoos, so I had a pretty good idea what one looked like. But the zoo birds were sluggish and dusty, and it had been difficult to make them out in the dim illumination of enclosures designed to simulate twilight. This bird was displayed to perfect advantage in my spotlight.

It was stunning. The kiwi's body, a round mass of fuzz, was about the size of a chicken's; it resembled a giant powder puff to which someone had attached the head of a snipe and the legs of a turkey. The eyes of the kiwi looked like black buttons, shiny and hard.

Forgetting my scientific duty to catch the bird, I stood and stared. The kiwi stood before me for a minute or more, trembling.

Looking closely, I saw that the kiwi had a poker bill, like that of a sandpiper, but longer and somewhat thicker. At the tip of the bill were nares, or nostrils. (Kiwi have a well-developed sense of smell; they use their beaks and olfactory apparatus, much like a mammal's, to locate invertebrate animals in soil.) The head was small and round, and long bristles grew from each corner of the mouth like cat's whiskers. The head connected directly to the torso, out of which legs sprouted—black, each thicker around than a man's thumb. The feet of the kiwi were big and clawed.

The kiwi's feathers were colored a fine wood-ash gray. All were delicately barred, as if they had been crosshatched in pencil.

Suddenly the kiwi turned and ran. I bolted after it but immediately became entangled in a thicket.

The kiwi was gone.

Although I was temporarily lost again, I was elated. Two of the goals of my original three-part quest had been satisfied. I had seen tuatara, hundreds upon hundreds of them. I had found a kiwi—as it happened, the rarest of the three species. Now my sights would be trained on one object alone. To find that object I would have to return to the mainland, for the Mercury islands are barren of frogs.

13.

Eastbourne.

Yesterday I attended a barbecue. The occasion was an informal gathering of the Society for Research on Amphibians and Reptiles in New Zealand (SRARNZ). It was a fairly new organization, and Charlie Daugherty was its president.

Dave Towns, a friendly, unassuming man who had led one of the landing parties in the Mercury islands, was the host. Charlie told me privately that Dave was widely regarded as New Zealand's foremost herpetologist.

Dave and his wife served me two plump sausages hot from the grill, then guided me to a room in which the others were already gathered. The man sitting next to me introduced himself as Jeff. He was slim, bearded, and perhaps thirty, and he talked with great enthusiasm about skinks. Skinks are lizards that live throughout the temperate and tropical world. In New Zealand there are twenty-one species, or so I had thought. Jeff was a lizard taxonomist. Several years of studying the native skinks, he said, had led him to conclude that there were more kinds of skinks in New Zealand than anyone had previously thought.

Intrigued, I asked him about Oliver's skink (*Cyclodina oliveri*), a lizard I had seen frequently on the Poor Knights. Oliver's skinks are slender, smooth-skinned, and several inches long. Their bodies are breadloaf-shaped in cross section.

Jeff smiled. "That's one of the lizards we've had to reconsider," he said. "Poor Knights *oliveri* are too different from other Oliver's skinks to consider them the same species. I'm afraid we'll be giving those a new name."

I couldn't resist asking about Whitaker's skink. Tony Whitaker, a legendary figure in New Zealand zoology and the lizard's namesake, was sipping beer within easy earshot. He was a tall, imposing man with piercing eyes and a long beard dabbed with gray. Tony heard the question and laughed. "Jeff wouldn't dare," he said.

As the evening progressed, I fished for information about frogs. The most helpful came from Alison Cree, my colleague on Stephens Island and the Poor Knights. Alison explained that she had done her Ph.D. work on the native amphibians. She knew exactly where I could find them.

Upon a sketch of the Coromandel Peninsula, Alison marked several locations. Each had frogs, she said, and one of the sites was inhabited by both North Island species—Hochstetter's and Archey's. "Spend a day, or perhaps just a few hours, in any one of these spots. Look under rocks, and I think you'll find what you're looking for. Of course you'll need a car. These places are a bit out of the way."

When I said that I would rent a car and visit the sites, Alison insisted that I make a solemn promise. "Don't divulge these locations to anyone. The frogs are scarce enough as it is, and giving away their hideaways might lead to disaster. Although the frogs are endangered, and there's a law against removing them from the wild, some people try to keep them as pets."

The barbecue broke up shortly afterward. Charlie and I drove the coast road home to Eastbourne, tracing the curves of bays and headlands. As we rounded a particularly sharp bend, a sign caught my eye. At first I thought it must be a joke. Drivers, the sign said, should be on the lookout for penguins.

14.

Rotorua.

I rented a Toyota in Wellington and headed north. Driving to the Coromandel Peninsula would take two days. My destination for the first day was Tongariro National Park, in central North Island.

For hours the highway ran through deep valleys and across broad plains. The landscape in all directions was covered with grass and sheep, or in plantations of radiata pine. Pastoral New Zealand had a remarkable sameness, I was continuing to find, that transcended every permutation in its landscape.

The towns along the way had Maori names that suggested the environment might not always have been so uniform. The most memorable were Tauherenikau, Kaiparoro, Pahiatua, Mangaonoho, and—my favorite, because I found it so pleasant to articulate—Eketahuna.

As the sun began to fade, I turned onto a dead-end road. It soon brought me up a steep grade to a place called Whakapapa Village, high in Tongariro Park. Near a grand old hotel known as the Chateau, built out of red brick, I found a motor camp and rented a tent site. A cold wind was blowing, and high above, wan sunlight the color of marmalade lingered on Mount Ruapehu, one of three volcanoes in the park.

In choosing economy over a warm and expensive room at the hotel, I made a near-fatal error. During the night a premature winter storm roared down the mountain. I had little cold-weather apparel, and the little that I had—three pairs of socks, two pairs of long johns, pants, a wool shirt, two sweaters, a down vest, a hat, mittens—I put on and wore inside my sleeping bag.

Minute by minute I shivered the agonizing night away, never sleeping, flinching each time the cold wind beat against my tent's flimsy nylon walls. I debated whether it was foolish to lie where I was, whether I should get up, climb out, and seek refuge. Eventually, just before sunup, the wind died. I crawled out of the tent. The tent was encrusted in ice, and all around it the grass was buried in snow.

Shivering violently, I dismantled the tent, threw it in the back of the car, and with the heater set on High, drove toward Rotorua. There, in a city famous for its hot mineral baths, I would catch up on sleep and melt the ice in my bones.

At Waiouru, in midmorning, I turned northward. For twenty-five miles I drove through flat, barren terrain unlike any other I had seen in New Zealand. Highway 1, as it runs up the east side of Tongariro Park, is known as the desert road. Driving it was like taking a brief holiday in the American Southwest. The soil was brown and bare, and the only birds I saw were starlings, magpies, and a lone harrier that circled lazily over the plain like a vulture. Enormous, big-shouldered towers of anthropomorphic steel lugged high-voltage lines toward opposite horizons, and there was a military base where soldiers of the New Zealand army executed marching drills behind barbed wire. The soil, the birds, the towers, the military men—all would have looked at home near Albuquerque or El Paso. To the west, the cones of the Tongariro volcanoes loomed like a mirage.

Near Turangi, out of the desert and back among green pastures, I stopped to visit a fish hatchery. There was little to see, save for hand-raised trout circling mechanically in gurgling pools, but the Tongariro River ran through the heart of the complex, and I wanted to get a look at it.

The Tongariro is among the world's best trout streams. For a century its imported, naturalized trout have lured fishermen from all over the world. In the 1980s Jimmy Carter waded the river and fished for its legendary rainbow trout. Zane Grey visited sixty years earlier, pursuing the same quarry.

Grey found the river's trout longer, plumper, and more numerous than any he had encountered elsewhere. In his book of New Zealand fishing, *Tales of an Angler's El Dorado*, he gushed:

> Tongariro! What a strange beautiful high-sounding name! It suited the noble river and the mountain from which it sprang. Tongariro! It was calling me. It would call to me across the vast lanes and leagues of the Pacific. It would draw me back again. Beautiful, green-white thundering Tongariro!

One gets the idea that Grey emerged from the river with a full creel.

In Turangi, a lakeside town catering shamelessly to fishermen, I parked near a motel named Angler's Paradise and set off in search of hot coffee. I found it in a tearoom that was part of an open-air shopping mall.

The place was empty but the coffee was hot, and I was happy to have a chance to read yesterday's *Auckland Herald*. An item on the front page caught my eye. "Pot Spotted," it said. There was a sketch of a tuatara, cupping a joint in the claws of one of its front feet. It was sprawled on its back in a forest of marijuana. Smoke mushroomed out of its nostrils.

Inside on page twenty was a headline: "Cannabis Found on Poor Knights." News of our most notable botanical discovery had apparently reached a big-city journalist.

From Turangi I drove north along the shore of Lake Taupo, a body of fresh water so large that it appeared to be an inland sea. There was no wind, and the lake's glassy surface formed a mirror in which the snow-crowned Tongariro volcanoes were reflected without a flaw.

The car rumbled onward. Humming to a Bing Crosby and Louis Armstrong duet on National Radio, I hurried through Taupo village, a crowded place full of tourists, motels, spas, boutiques, and Kentucky Fried Chicken. Soon afterward I passed the Wairakei Station, a geothermal generating plant that is among the biggest in the world. At midafternoon I coasted from a high ridge into the Rotorua basin. The radio was reporting on the stock market. Good prices, I learned, were being fetched for cattle and pigs.

Within minutes of arriving in Rotorua I had secured a room in a B&B, scalded myself in a hot shower, and fallen profoundly asleep.

That night I dreamed about frogs. I awoke just before six.

15.

Thames.

I was desperate. I had been turning mossy rocks on a humid, jungle-swathed mountainside for hours, and the only slimy skin I had seen was my own. I was caked with mud. I was raked with scratches. There were no frogs.

Alison had provided me with driving instructions that were clear and accurate. I had climbed high up the spine of the Coromandel Peninsula, following roads hacked into the precipitous walls of deep, bush-choked valleys. Kauri trees were numerous, their boles and crowns nearly as titanic as those I'd seen in the Waipoa Forest. Alison had said I would find a pull-off in a particular place, and I did. Soon, on a narrow walking track, I was ascending a steep grade into the bush.

After hiking for a quarter of an hour, I had not found the rock pile that Alison said I would find a few minutes from the road. There had been a few scattered rocks, but none in congregation. I continued onward, thinking that the distance covered in "a few minutes" at Alison's brisk pace might require a half hour at mine.

The trail climbed steeply. Every few minutes I paused to gasp for breath, or to roll a solitary rock, until I emerged from the shadows in brilliant sunshine. To the west I could see mountainsides thick with kauri and tree ferns, and beyond, a sheet of sparkling blue water. The water, known as the Firth of Thames, stretched for miles—south, west, and north. Somewhere along its far shore, concealed by haze, lay Auckland.

Alison's directions had made no mention of a viewpoint. I retraced my steps back down the mountain, into the bush. In ten minutes I came to a place that, from a new angle, looked something like a rock pile.

I rolled, and carefully replaced, a hundred chunks of moss-covered stone. Because of a drought, the ground was dry beneath them. This was not encouraging. Frogs—even terrestrial frogs—need moisture. It seemed likely that those living here had retreated deep into the talus, seeking dampness. Finding them might prove impossible, I realized, no matter how hard and long I searched.

At noon I rested and ate a picnic lunch. I was in low spirits and cursed my luck. Having seen hundreds of tuatara and gotten a close look at a kiwi, I was at last in a forest where native frogs were abundant. If I could find one, the goal I had set for myself years before would have been achieved. But the secretive amphibians continued to deny me satisfaction. In Alison's rock pile I had discovered only worms, spiders, pill bugs, and land snails.

After finishing my sandwich I decided, before conceding defeat, to search for one more hour.

Fifty minutes passed. Then, beneath a rock the size of a breadbox, I noticed a shape. It was the snout of a small animal. Looking closely, I could see a pair of golden eyes and glistening skin that was mottled green and brown. From its nostrils to its blunt posterior, the creature's length was about an inch.

I looked closely. There were three of the animals, and there was no doubt that they were frogs!

The frogs were perfectly camouflaged, and I had mistaken them at first for bits of earth and stone. A distinct ridge swept back from each of their eyes, identifying them as *Leiopelma archeyi*, or Archey's frogs. I looked at their tiny feet. No webbing filled the spaces between the toes. I concede that Archey's frogs—superficially, anyhow—are not creatures most people would find interesting. They are practically invisible, lack external ears, rarely make noises, and spend their lives hiding in rock piles. Scientists, however, find Archey's frogs compelling subjects of study.

The frogs possess tail-wagging muscles—no tails, mind you, just the muscles to wag them if they had. Biologists studying the development of the vertebrates are intrigued by these muscles, because frogs are thought to have evolved from salamanderlike creatures with tails. During their evolution, frogs—with the exception of four species—lost their tails and the muscles that moved them.

Three of the four primitive frogs that retain tail-wagging muscles live in New Zealand. The fourth, *Ascaphus trueii*, lives in the northwestern United States and Canada. Long ago, anatomical similarities between the North American frog and the New Zealand amphibians led scientists to assume that they were closely related. In Wellington, Charlie had told me that recent studies (using a sophisticated analytical process call electrophoresis) had borne out the suspicion.

That certain frogs in New Zealand and North America can be more closely related to each other than to amphibians in their own hemispheres is an astounding zoogeographical fact. Frogs cannot survive at sea on rafts of driftwood, moving from island to island and continent to continent, as lizards can. Their tender skin cannot tolerate extremes of salt and sun. The distribution of the family *Leiopelmatidae* is not explainable in terms of natural expansion and colonization.

Geologists find tail-wagging frogs no less intriguing than do herpetologists. The present distribution of the amphibians is among the most convincing pieces of evidence supporting the theory of plate tectonics and continental drift. The frogs are so primitive, so ancient in origin, that they date to a time when much of the world's dry land was fused into a single supercontinent. When that vast landmass broke up, populations of tailed frogs sailed away from each other on newly formed islands and continents. Time passed—two hundred million years, give or take an epoch. Now there are four survivors, three of them far removed from the fourth.

Archey's frogs were not described until 1942, although S. P. Smith had found them on Coromandel's Tokatea Ridge as early as 1862. E. G. Turbott named them *Leiopelma archeyi* after Sir Gilbert Archey. (Sir Gilbert had written a description of the frog's reproductive habits in 1922.) Archey's frogs live only on Coromandel, in humid forests between 600 and 3,300 feet elevation. Unlike more typical frogs found in America and elsewhere, they reproduce on land, under rocks. The females lay the eggs in clusters, and the males guard them until tiny four-legged frogs emerge. Unlike most of their kin outside of New Zealand, the frogs do not enter the world as free-roaming tadpoles. Evolution—or a lack of it—has deprived the Archey's frog of a traditional amphibian childhood.

One at a time, I picked up the frogs. I gazed into their eyes and watched the delicate skin of their throats flutter as they breathed. Within a minute, warmed by my hands, each grew restless and jumped.

A feeling of peace crept over me. At last I had completed the zoological flush—had clawed, climbed, negotiated, and otherwise wriggled myself into proximity with the three animals I had been seeking. For the first time during the course of my New Zealand travels, I felt I could relax.

Only a few days remained before my flight to America.

16.

Auckland.

A few hours after finding the frogs, I checked into a room in the Brian Boru Hotel in the small, bustling city of Thames.

Thames occupies a narrow flat on the eastern shore of the Firth of Thames. It is an odd town—a minor tourist mecca which, in turning its attentions inland to the Coromandel hills, largely ignores its waterfront.

Walking through the center of town, I found the main thoroughfare crowded with automobiles. Between the road and the water I found a derelict railroad yard and a sandy field strewn with rusting iron. Farther on, tied alongside a pier, were a fleet of abandoned and rotting wooden boats. But east of the main road, toward the interior, Thames seemed to be prospering. There, beneath marquees in which house sparrows nested, I found a miniature Earl's Court—a place of crowded sidewalks, bottle shops, groceries, restaurants, and tearooms. I bought a newspaper and an apple and sat on a bench, thinking to myself that the town was more revealing of the men and women who had built it than of the environment in which it was placed.

I left Thames the following morning. Driving west toward Hamilton, I passed through miles of grazing country. One view looked much the same as the next until, in a green valley identical to a dozen others I had seen, I found a factory spewing dense, malodorous smoke. It stung my eyes and spurred me onward.

In Hamilton I stopped at a McDonald's to buy coffee. The place swarmed with teenagers. Searching for the men's room, I discovered a sign: "If vandalism continues, we will have no choice but to close the restrooms to the public."

The day was gloomy. Thick clouds hung low in the sky, threatening rain, and the country west of the city was flat and bleak—Kansas displaced. I was not surprised when a sign along the road pointed toward a Mormon temple.

"Private Road, Visitors Welcome," the sign said. Curious about what the Church of Jesus Christ of Latter-day Saints might be up to in New Zealand, I drove ahead. I came to a stop beside a whitewashed brick tower. Beside the building was a parking lot, and beyond it stood a low, glass-fronted building marked "Visitor Center." Inside I met Sister Ellis.

A slender, attractive American woman clad in an unbecoming black dress, Sister Ellis responded to my request for a tour of the temple with a look of mild shock. Then she composed herself, explaining that the temple, a sacred place, was off limits to visitors. If I wanted a tour, she said, she would provide one of the visitor center.

The centerpiece of the modern concrete building was a statue of a resurrected, well-scrubbed Jesus, grotesquely oversized and replete with gaping nail wounds. Jesus' face wore a vacant expression, as if he was bored. "The statue was brought here," Sister Ellis explained, "all the way from Italy."

The walls were hung with backlit panels of the sort used to display main courses and desserts in American steak houses. Each featured an important moment in the life of Jesus. The Israelites in the depictions had skin that was wholesomely pink, as if they had just stepped from a bath. Their clothes, clean and neatly pressed, appeared to be new or freshly laundered.

The tour concluded in an adjacent room beside another backlit panel. It showed a room in which the walls and ceiling were painted white and the floor was covered in thick pile carpet. The carpet was white, and so were the sturdy upholstered chairs distributed upon it.

Sister Ellis handed me a complimentary paperback edition of the *Book of Mormon*. According to its author, Joseph Smith, Junior, the book was based on a set of golden plates found in my home state of New York during the nineteenth century. The plates were covered with inscriptions in a strange language, but with divine guidance Smith was able to translate them. Later the plates vanished, and Smith was martyred, but "God made sure," said Sister Ellis, "that Joseph Smith's translation of the texts survived." Grateful for the book, whatever its contents, and groping for proper thanks, I asked Sister Ellis about the white room on the illuminated panel.

"This is a room in the temple," she said. "It is a place where important ceremonies are held. We believe that this room is much like what we will find in heaven. We go there, in the presence of our elders, to prepare ourselves for the Lord."

I stepped outside into a chilling rain, put the car into gear, and drove away deep in thought. Although a white room with sturdy furniture and wall-to-wall carpeting was Sister Ellis's idea of heaven, it wasn't mine. If, somewhere above, a better world than ours awaits the righteous, I picture it as a place where the weather is warm all year, where plants grow in profusion with never a drought or deluge, where the air is scented with flowers, and the forest teems with songbirds and animals of rare beauty. With this fantasy in mind, I did something the good sister could never do: I took out a map and drove there.

When I arrived, Peter had just returned from his garden

with a handful of parsley. I had hoped he would be pleased to see me; he was, and insisted that I stay for tea.

Upon leaving the temple, I had stopped at the first bottle shop along the highway and bought a bottle of Glenfiddich. Now I produced it. "Ed, you shouldn't have," said Peter, "but thank heaven you did."

Peter, during each of my visits, drank whiskey the way some people take the eucharist—ceremoniously, never in a hurry. He was no drunkard. Until it was empty he worked on a bottle steadily, over the course of a day and night, but I never saw him inebriated.

When Peter offered to pour me a glass, I accepted. I diluted the amber fluid with a dash of hot water, as he did, toasted the distiller, and drank.

Time was running out. Soon I would board a flight to Los Angeles, but more immediately, Peter would be serving evening tea. "Ed, I'm all right here. Hurry, and you can pay a final visit to Fairyland. After we have our pudding and coffee, it will be too dark."

I walked confidently down the tracks, knowing exactly which turns to take, which slopes to descend. Four years ago, exploring the bush during my first visit, I had taken nearly an hour to find my way to the grotto. This time I reached Fairyland in minutes.

I stayed as long as I dared. I listened to the water trickling over the rocks, drank in the earthy vesper fragrance of the jungle, gazed into the living thatch of fern fronds and palm leaves overhead, and listened to the song of the riroriro.

Tea that last night at Peter's consisted of fillet steaks, fresh cauliflower, garden potatoes, and sliced fresh tomatoes, all bathed in gravy. Pudding (the course Americans call dessert) followed—sliced pears and fresh whipped cream.

Until midnight Peter and I stayed up talking, coaxing the

whiskey from the bottle. It felt like old times. On my parting night here four years ago, I never dreamed I would return. I had come back—twice.

"Tell me, Ed, will you ever come again, or have we seen the last of you in New Zealand?" Phrasing the question, drawing on a hand-rolled cigarette beneath a faded photograph of a sailing ship, his free hand resting beside a glass of whiskey, Peter fit the storybook image of an old sailor. A parrot on his shoulder would have added nothing.

I found myself thinking, If only New Zealand wasn't so damned far away. If only it wasn't so expensive to reach. Then I came to my senses. The distance and the expense made the country the place that it is. No nation of comparable size in the world is so isolated. No one, come to think of it, hoped New Zealand remained isolated more than I.

Two years before, during a flight from Honolulu to Auckland, I sat beside a lawyer from Missoula, Montana. He was a fly fisherman and was going to South Island to cast for trout. When I asked if he had been to New Zealand before, he laughed.

"I made my first trip to New Zealand many years ago," he said. "I wanted to see if the fishing was all it's made out to be." He paused and broke into a grin. "This is my seventh visit."

*Y*es," I told Peter. A few minutes later I stepped outside to commune with nature and the tree ferns. The Southern Cross was stretched across the sky, and in the bush a morepork was calling.

EPILOGUE

On the thirteenth of September, 1990, the British journal *Nature* brought the scientific world stunning news: Analysis of blood samples collected during the 1988–89 research program revealed that the tuatara, singular, is in fact tuatara, *plural*. There are two species. The first, *Sphenodon punctatus*, the one I saw and the one zoologists have long acknowledged, lives on all the tuatara islands except one. The second, to be known as *S. guntheri*, after Albert Gunther, the scientist at the British Museum who first brought the unusual pedigree of the tuatara to light, inhabits a single island of less than ten acres in the Cook Strait.

The discovery is something of a vindication for nineteenth-century zoologists. A century ago, the tuatara of the island—it is known as the North Brother—were recognized as a unique species. Later, the similarity in appearance among all tuatara was used in argument against the existence of a second species, and the two varieties were merged into a single entity.

Suddenly, Gunther's tuatara (to coin a common name for a beast without one) has been resurrected. Credit for the miracle must go to the *Nature* article's four authors: Charlie Daugherty, Alison Cree, Mike Thompson, and Jennie Hay, a student with whom I traveled to the Mercury islands. Their work has given the world a new species—doubled, in fact, the number of living ambassadors of the order *Sphenodontida*—at a time when we are losing other species fast. An important zoological discovery, the rebirth of Gunther's tuatara is cause for rejoicing.

Two weeks and two days before the world got its new tuatara, it lost a good man. On the twenty-eighth of August, 1990, an hour and a half past midnight with several hours to go before sunup, Peter Malcolm Miller was snug in his bunk when a stroke ended his life. In the rustic cabin built by his father in 1924, surrounded by his seven beloved acres of bush, the old sailor embarked on life's final voyage.

INDEX

Mormon Church, 225–26

Mountain daisy (*Gelmisia coriacea*), 71

Mount Balloon, 71

Mount Cook, 4

Mount Cook lily (*Ranunculus lyalli*), 71

Mount Egmont, 97–98

Mount Hart, 71

Mount Ruapehu, 217

Murderer's Bay, 10

Myna bird, 159

Nettle plant (*Urtica ferox*), 110–11

Newman, Don, 46–47

Newton, John, 173, 191

New Zealand, xi–xiii
  exports of, xii, 15
  fauna and flora of, 4–8
  geography and climate of, 1–4
  history, politics, and economy of, 8–16
  human habitation of, xiv, 5, 8–15
  maps of, xvi, xvii

New Zealand Company, 11

New Zealand Department of Conservation, 194

New Zealand Wildlife Service, 99, 117, 120, 194

Ngatamariki sheep station, 36–41

Nikau tree, 4

Norfolk Island pine tree, 163

North Cape, 1

North Island, xvi (map), 2

Oban village, 75, 83–85

Oliver's skink (*Cyclodina oliveri*), 214–15

Owen, Richard, 79, 105

Palmer, Stanley, 174–75, 191

Parakeet, 64, 120

Parata, George, 169, 174, 187

Parrish, Richard, 173

Patterson Inlet, 75, 81

Penguin, 42–44, 54, 55–56

Petrel (bird), 47, 109, 116, 195

Picton, 50

Pigeon, 23

Pigs, importation of, 25

Piha, 97, 147, 150–60

Place names, xiv–xv, 2

Plate tectonics, 4, 6, 222–23

Pohutukawa tree (*Metrosideros excelsa*), 90

Poor Knights Islands, 144
  Maori abandonment of, 169
  tuatara research project on, 169, 172–76, 182–84

Poor Knights lily (*Xeronema callistemon*), 177

Port Nicholson, 12, 43

Puriri tree fern, 178

Queen Charlotte Sound, 48–50

Radiata pine tree, 33

Railroads, 50, 52, 82–83

Rakiura. *See* Stewart Island

Rangitoto Island, 172–73

Rats, 5, 8, 197–98, 204–205

234